W9-AXF-968

Twayne's United States Authors Series

Sylvia E. Bowman, *Editor*

INDIANA UNIVERSITY

Delmore Schwartz

DELMORE SCHWARTZ

DELMORE SCHWARTZ

By RICHARD MC DOUGALL

 243

Twayne Publishers, Inc.　::　New York

Copyright © 1974 by Twayne Publishers, Inc.

All Rights Reserved

Library of Congress Cataloging in Publication Data

McDougall, Richard.
　　Delmore Schwartz.

　　(Twayne's United States authors series, TUSAS 243)
　　Bibliography:　p.143
　　1.　Schwartz, Delmore, 1913–1966
PS3537.C79Z77　　　　　　818'.5'209　　　　　73–17285
ISBN 0–8057–0657–7

MANUFACTURED IN THE UNITED STATES OF AMERICA

PS
3537
.C79
Z77

751971

For

DAN AND JAN HEIPLE

with hope

Dexter Library
Northland College
Ashland, Wisconsin 54806

Preface

Delmore Schwartz thought of himself as being a poet of alienation, a witness to various forms of spiritual isolation in the modern world—as a Jew, as an artist, and as a human being. This role was one that he felt the circumstances of his life had assigned him to play. "Alienation" has become a stock term by now, yet I believe myself that it describes an abiding condition of modern life, especially for poets.

Schwartz's obsession with exile and estrangement was accompanied by a longing for unity and communion. The drama of his work as a whole, as I shall try to show in this book, arises from the interaction of the two: his awareness of loneliness and his reaching out for oneness. In many of his later poems he tries to break away from his earlier role of isolated intellectual, to abandon an extremely conscious and reflective attitude toward life, for the sake of a symbolic—perhaps a mystical—celebration of a kind of perception that he calls "summer knowledge." In particular, he changes in his understanding of what the role of the artist should be. Formally, he moves away from the rigorously organized poems of his youth toward a freer verse characterized by the incantatory rhythms of the celebrant and seer. On the level of symbolism, he shows a coherent pattern of development and transformation that unites the imagery of his early and late work.

In many instances, however, he adumbrates rather than realizes his intentions. There was a tragic disorder in Schwartz's personal life that kept him from full development as a poet. This study tends to show, therefore, his work under two aspects: what he attempted and what he actually achieved. His achievement, though considerable, is haunted by forsaken possibilities.

Chapter 1 presents some biographical findings to accompany the Chronology and summarizes Schwartz's writing career, with emphasis upon his uncollected work. Chapter 2 touches upon the phenomenon of alienation, specifically the isolation of poets in the modern world, as Schwartz himself describes it in some of his critical articles and in his own words, as distinct from the words of his fictional personae in his stories and poems. In the latter part of this chapter, I consider Schwartz's concept of himself as a Jew, and his attitude toward Jewish experience as an influence upon his work. Chapter 3 outlines what I think are his main preoccupations: his concern with selfhood, with time and consciousness, and with spiritual transcendence; his devotion to culture and "culture heroes"; and his portrayal of the city, New York, as the ground of spiritual exile. The remaining five chapters discuss his most important work in detail and in largely chronological order. Although it does not have a section of its own I often refer to Schwartz's criticism, especially as it relates to his practice, as in Chapter 2. In addition, the list of selected critical articles and reviews in the bibliography contains a brief annotation on each.

I am happy to have had the help and encouragement of a number of Schwartz's friends, associates, and admirers of his work. I thank Gertrude Buckman and Elizabeth Pollet Rosengarten; James Laughlin, his friend and publisher throughout his career; Harry Levin, William Phillips, Meyer Schapiro, and Maurice Zolotow; Kenneth Henry, one of Schwartz's first students at Harvard, with whom I had a helpful discussion of his work; Merrill T. Leffler, whose detailed bibliography was indispensable; Leonard S. Reiss, for providing me with a copy of *The Poets' Pack*, containing some of Schwartz's student work; Louis Simon and Roger W. Straus, Jr.; and for their friendly interest, Erin Clermont, Babette Deutsch, David H. Greene, Irving Howe, Heinz Politzer, M. L. Rosenthal, and I. A. Salomon. I was also helped by numerous correspondents at universities with which the poet was associated, especially by Donald A. Dike of Syracuse University and by Neill Foote and Margaret Griffin of the Department of Philosophy of Harvard.

RICHARD MC DOUGALL

Acknowledgments

I thank the publishers of the following works for permission to reprint excerpts from them.

From Delmore Schwartz, *In Dreams Begin Responsibilities* and *Summer Knowledge: New and Selected Poems, 1938–1958*, copyright 1938 by New Directions Publishing Corporation; Delmore Schwartz, *Shenandoah*, copyright 1941 by New Directions Publishing Corporation; Delmore Schwartz, *Genesis: Book I*, copyright 1943 by New Directions Publishing Corporation; Delmore Schwartz, *The World Is a Wedding*, copyright 1948 by Delmore Schwartz; Delmore Schwartz, *Vaudeville for a Princess and Other Poems*, copyright 1950 by New Directions Publishing Corporation; Jean-Paul Sartre, *Baudelaire*, translated by Martin Turnell, copyright 1950 by New Directions Publishing Corporation; an excerpt from a letter of May 8, 1969 by James Laughlin to the author. Excerpts from all of the above are reprinted by permission of New Directions Publishing Corporation and James Laughlin. Grateful acknowledgment is made to the publisher for the use of the photograph of Delmore Schwartz that appears on the jacket of this book.

From Delmore Schwartz, *Summer Knowledge: New and Selected Poems, 1938–1958*. Copyright 1959 by Doubleday and Company, Inc. Reprinted by permission of Doubleday and Company, Inc.

From James Joyce, *Dubliners*. Originally published by B. W. Huebsch, Inc. in 1916. Copyright © 1967 by the Estate of James Joyce. Reprinted by permission of The Viking Press, Inc.

From Max Brod, *Franz Kafka: A Biography*. Copyright 1947, © 1960 by Schocken Books Inc. Reprinted by permission of Schocken Books Inc.

From Leslie A. Fiedler, *Waiting for the End*. Copyright 1964 by Leslie A. Fiedler. Reprinted by permission of Stein and Day, Publishers.

From T. S. Eliot, "Animula" and "Gerontion," from his *Col-

lected Poems 1909–1962 (1963). Reprinted by permission of Harcourt Brace Johanovich, Inc.

From Wallace Stevens, *Letters of Wallace Stevens,* edited by Holly Stevens (1966). Reprinted by permission of Alfred A. Knopf, Inc.

From John Berryman, *Short Poems* (1967). Reprinted by permission of Farrar, Straus and Giroux, Inc.

I also wish to thank:

The editor of *Poetry* for permission to quote from the following articles: Delmore Schwartz, "The Critical Method of R. P. Blackmur," "The Vocation of the Poet in the Modern World," and "T. S. Eliot's Voice and His Voices"; Philip Blair Rice, "The Rimbaud Mystery Clarified"; and Hayden Carruth, "Comment." Copyright 1938; 1951; 1954 and 1955; 1940; and 1968, respectively, by The Modern Poetry Association.

The Macmillan Publishing Co., Inc., in acknowledgment of my use of the epigraphs that precede *Responsibilities* by William Butler Yeats, in his *Collected Poems* (1952).

Philip Rahv for permission to quote from his article, "Delmore Schwartz: The Paradox of Precocity," which appeared in the *New York Review of Books,* May 20, 1971.

Contents

Chronology

1913   Delmore David Schwartz born December 8 in Brooklyn, New York, the first of two sons of Harry and Rose (Nathanson) Schwartz.

1927-1931   Attended high schools in Manhattan, where the family had moved. Graduated from George Washington High School in the Washington Heights section.

1931-1932   Attended University of Wisconsin as a freshman.

1932-1935   Attended New York University, Washington Square College. Graduated with a Bachelor of Arts degree in philosophy.

1935-1937   Graduate student of philosophy, Harvard University. Studied with Alfred N. Whitehead, Ralph B. Perry and William E. Hocking, among others; received outstanding grades. However, left Harvard without taking a degree in March, 1937; lived thereafter in New York City. Began to publish in magazines: criticism, poetry, and fiction.

1938   In June, married Gertrude Buckman, a friend from high school years. First collection, *In Dreams Begin Responsibilities.*

1939-1940   Residence at the writer's colony, Yaddo, Saratoga Springs, New York, from the fall of 1939 to the spring of 1940. Awarded Guggenheim Fellowship in 1940 (as again in 1941). Appointed Briggs-Copeland Instructor of English Composition at Harvard, assuming position in the fall semester, 1940. Translation of Arthur Rimbaud's *Saison en Enfer* published 1939 and again in second edition, 1940.

1940-1947   Harvard years, residence in Cambridge. Taught courses in composition and advanced writing. During the early 1940's was informally associated with New Directions, at that time located in Cambridge. Much magazine publication. *Shenandoah* (1941), *Genesis* (1943). In 1943 became an editor of the *Partisan Review*, with which he remained until 1955. Divorced in 1944. In the same year appointed Briggs-Copeland Assistant Professor of English Composition. Resigned position in August, 1947, a year before the expiration of his appointment, for reasons not officially stated, but probably in part because of dissatisfaction with his university career.

1948   *The World Is a Wedding.*

1949- In June, 1949, married the writer Elizabeth Pollet. Resided
1957   in Greenwich Village, New York City, and later, from 1952
until 1957, when he and his wife separated, in Baptistown,
New Jersey, in the country, which probably had considerable
influence upon his later poetry. During this period held
numerous positions as a visiting lecturer at various universities,
including: Princeton, academic year 1949-1950, as a lecturer
on T. S. Eliot for the Christian Gauss Seminars in Criticism,
known at the time as the Princeton Seminars in Literary
Criticism; Kenyon School of English, Kenyon College, summer session, 1950; Indiana School of Letters, Indiana University (a continuation of the Kenyon School of English), summer
session, 1951, during which he gave a course on William
Butler Yeats and T. S. Eliot; University of Chicago, spring
quarter, 1954, with courses in creative writing and modern
poetry. *Vaudeville for a Princess* (1950). During 1952 and
1953 was on the advisory board of *Perspectives USA*, a quarterly established by the Ford Foundation and published by
James Laughlin. At the same time, was consultant for New
Directions. Won awards from *Poetry* in 1950 (as again in
1959), and from the National Institute of Arts and Letters
in 1953. Poetry editor and film critic of the *New Republic*,
1955-1957.

1959   *Summer Knowledge: New and Selected Poems, 1938-1958.*
1960   Awarded the Bollingen Prize in Poetry for 1959 and the
Shelley Memorial Prize.
1961   *Successful Love and Other Stories.*
1962- Visiting Professor of English at Syracuse University. Taught
1965   fiction writing and courses in literature.
1966   Delmore Schwartz died on July 11 in New York City.

CHAPTER 1

"His Endless Guilt, His Passion for the Snow"

from "The Masters of the Heart Touched the Unknown"

THE numerous memoirs about Delmore Schwartz show that he had the power to obsess not only his friends but even those who were hardly more than chance acquaintances. A legend has formed around his name, one that he himself fostered in his lifetime, especially in his work that shows an image of himself in the mirror of art. In essence, the legend is that of a young American poet and intellectual who came of age in the America of the Depression years and emerged suddenly and precociously from a culturally indifferent, middle-class, Jewish milieu. Schwartz's life and work were decisively influenced by the conflicts and anomalies inherent in this rise with its attendant estrangement from his own family and from society as a whole.

He is remembered above all for his intelligence, which reveals itself in all of his writing, critical and poetic. He also had a quick sense of humor that lightened his intellectual earnestness and often took the form of genial mockery of himself and others. Beneath the playful surface, however, which Philip Rahv believes was the aspect of him that his casual acquaintances saw and remembered, there lay an essentially somber personality—"sardonic," as Rahv calls it—only too well known by his intimate friends, for which the humor often served, it would seem, as a defensive social mask.[1] Schwartz was a deeply disturbed, self-doubting, inwardly dwelling man of marked egoism and self-concern. His despondency eventually passed beyond the borders of sanity into actual madness, which was diagnosed as having been both manic-depressive and paranoid.

Despite his illness, Schwartz in his best work never gave way

15

to irrationality. Alfred Kazin remarks that "the extraordinary thing about Delmore as a man and a writer is that he was never dominated by the familiar claims for 'madness,' for surrender.... He lived by intellectual tradition, by philosophy and reason, by a boundless faith in the great creative figures of modern literature and art.... Delmore the poet believed in nothing so much as the virtue and reason of poetry...."[2]

Nevertheless, Schwartz's illness is reflected in much of his writing. One is often aware of an indefinable malaise, an unfocused sense of guilt, a pervasive anxiety and fear, as well as an obsessive concern with events and circumstances that are past and beyond help. Moreover, his emotional bias caused him to dwell upon the alienation of the individual, especially the poet, in modern society. But it would be wrong to approach his work with the preconception that, since he was ill, his work is suspect. At their best, Schwartz's creative work and his criticism show a wholeness of vision and a soundness of judgment that put both on the side of sanity and light. By formal means, by means of art, he was able to transcend his bias and to present a vision of modern life that has a wide relevance.

I   *The Family Influence*

Schwartz's family life when he was a child and a young man was a major source of his unhappiness, and it appears in his work in its fictional transformations as a focal point for his meditations on various forms of estrangement and antagonism. There can be no doubt that his childhood was affected for the worse by the incompatible marriage of his mother and father, the origins of which he portrays in what is probably his most powerful short story. "In Dreams Begin Responsibilities."

Of Rumanian origin, Schwartz's parents emigrated with their families to the United States while still young children. Schwartz's father, like some of the fathers in his work, was a businessman driven by the ambition to become rich. His business was real estate, and he was apparently unscrupulous in some of his methods. During the prosperous years before the Depression, he did in fact become rich—only to die at the beginning of the economic crisis. A bank, which became his trustee, indifferently allowed his estate to deteriorate; and

Schwartz, who had expected to inherit a considerable amount of money, came of age in poverty. The event undoubtedly affected his work: the Depression appears as the most significant fact in his early stories. Economic failure has blighted the lives of his characters, frustrating the sensitive and intelligent, giving the lie to the ambitions of the materialistic.

Schwartz is said to have admired his father, despite obvious differences in their personal aims, and to have hated his mother, to whom it appears he was nevertheless emotionally bound. The ambivalent relationship is reflected in his work, notably in *Coriolanus and His Mother*, in which the ghost of Sigmund Freud himself analyzes the Roman hero's thralldom to the matron Volumnia. Mrs. Schwartz did not share her son's interests, and no evidence exists that she recognized or praised his talent. She and his father separated when the poet was still young, and they were finally divorced after considerable reluctance on her part. The struggles between Michael and Sarah in the story "The Child Is the Meaning of This Life" and between Hershey Green's parents in *Genesis* are doubtless fictional portrayals of their marriage. Schwartz was close to his younger brother, Kenneth, and to his maternal grandmother, who possibly was the model for Ruth Hart in the story.

II   *The Final Phase*

The Chronology of this book provides the external details of Schwartz's life to about 1957. Thereafter, the picture becomes increasingly obscure and difficult to trace. By this time, Schwartz had entered the final phase of his life, years of loneliness marked by quarrels with his friends and general decline. Except for his time in Syracuse, New York, where he stayed for several months after resigning from the university, he lived in New York City, mostly in Greenwich Village. On occasion he was committed to hospitals. By this time he had become the victim of elaborate delusions of persecution; and he imagined that his friends and former students were united in a conspiracy to destroy him. His paranoia was worsened by addiction to tranquilizers, to other drugs, and to heavy drinking. Like Dylan Thomas before him, Schwartz frequented Village bars where he talked endlessly with strangers and played the role—against his better self—of the alcoholic, self-destructive poet. He was at a

far remove from his earlier years; for according to Maurice
Zolotow, his friend and fellow student at the University of Wisconsin, Schwartz as a young man did not drink at all. There is
evidence, however, that the illness that was to destroy him was
already present in latent form.

Schwartz spent the final months of his life in almost unbroken
isolation, living in hotels in the midtown area of the city, off
Broadway. His last room, which he occupied three months
before his death, was in the Columbia Hotel on West Forty-
sixth Street, one of the many nondescript and forlorn lodgings
for transients in the theater district. He died there of a heart
attack early in the morning of Monday, July 11, 1966. His funeral
service, held on the following Monday, was attended by many
of the friends from whom he had separated himself but who
had not allowed themselves to be separated from him. He was
buried the same day in a cemetery in Westwood, New Jersey.

III   A Survey of Work

Schwartz's first published work, four poems, appeared in a
collection of students' verse, The Poets' Pack, issued in 1932 by
the George Washington High School. At this time, there was
considerable interest at the school in writing poetry because
of one of Schwartz's English teachers, Mary J. J. Wrinn, who
taught classes in the craft and was the adviser of a poetry club.
Harper and Brothers published her Hollow Reed in 1935, a book
on poetry writing in which she used as examples the work of
her students as well as famous poems. It contains three of
Schwartz's contributions to The Poets' Pack and two other
poems of his.[3]

This early work is not particularly outstanding or much superior to the work of Miss Wrinn's other students, none of whom
became poets, as far as it is known. The influence of Hart Crane
appears in Schwartz's "Automobile": "O brutal plunge, stern
prodigy of stuff/ Too foreign to ourselves and separate—/ Your
lithe, steel-cradled force is not enough."[4] "The Saxophone," an
impression of New York City that uses jazz imagery, anticipates
later work about the metropolis:

> This sobbing fits the city—can't you see,
> Listening to that croon, a sprawling drunkard

Under the leprous light of dimming lamp-posts
As day flows in between the tall, tall buildings.[5]

"Washington Bridge, December 1929" also refers to New York. "E.A.P.—A Portrait," and "Saturday's Child" are like the other poems—the work of a novice in love with poetry but not yet wholly a poet.

In 1934, two years after *The Poets' Pack*, Schwartz published two poems in *Mosaic*, a short-lived little magazine of which he was an associate editor—"Aubade," a trivial lyric, and "The Beautiful American Word, Sure," a fluent and graceful sonnet that was collected in *In Dreams Begin Responsibilities*. In 1936, while at Harvard, he contributed a short play in prose and verse, *Choosing Company*, to an annual of the time, *The New Caravan*. A slight work never reprinted, it is interesting only because it contains images and ideas that Schwartz developed later, including his ambivalent attitude toward the value of consciousness. It is "the key of things, the light of the world."[6] Yet the hero of the play is told: "...your actual gaze will never meet/ Your heart, the stuff in your limbs is dark/ beneath you...."[7] This opposition between the light of consciousness and the darkness of existence is at the heart of all of Schwartz's future work.

In the same year, 1936, Harvard awarded Schwartz a Bowdoin Prize in the humanities for his essay, "Poetry as Imitation," an exuberantly ambitious attempt to define poetry as a form of cognition.[8] Its point of departure is Aristotle's statement in his *Poetics* that poetry is imitation and a passage in the philosopher's "treatise on the soul," *De Anima*, in which he "describes the mind's act, when it knows, in such a way that a kind of identity seems to exist between the act of knowledge and the act of imitation. The mind when it knows 'becomes' the object which it knows...." As an example, "...the intellect, when it knows the triangularity of a triangle, becomes at the moment merely that meaning, triangularity." This becoming the object is imitation. "If the artist also imitates, is not knowledge of some variety also the product?... *The act of writing a poem is an act of knowing....*"[9] Though Schwartz would no doubt have applied this definition to all poetry, it is particularly applicable to the kind of poetry that he himself was to write, in which the intellect plays an active part. Like the statement of theme in *Choosing Company*, it anticipates the future in very brief form.

In describing what is known by means of poetry, as distinguished from "what is known by means of philosophy and science," Schwartz also brings in what is to become a major image in his work, "the simple metaphor of the looking-glass," which "shows that some things can be known in only one way. Only by looking in the mirror . . . can I know what my face 'looks like.' . . . Just in this way . . . we need some mirror to see our disguised emotions and motives and to see our feelings from the outside, 'objectively.' . . . That mirror is Art. . . . The medium of each art is the looking-glass which by imitation shows us what we could not see in any other way."[10]

Schwartz began to publish frequently after he won the Bowdoin Prize. In December, 1937, the *Partisan Review* published his best-known story, "In Dreams Begin Responsibilities."[11] This also appeared in James Laughlin's *New Directions in Prose and Poetry 1937*, an annual of new writing in a series that began in the preceding year and continues at present. The story was accompanied in the collection by "The Commencement Day Address," a philosophical speech by a Professor Duspenser before the graduating class of a college in New York City. The professor is one of the father figures that appear in several of Schwartz's earlier pieces, and who represent the claims of consciousness. The speech is studded with lines that Schwartz extracted from his poems, including "In the Naked Bed, in Plato's Cave." Of the three poems also published in the 1937 issue of the annual, two of them, "At This Moment of Time" and "O Love, Sweet Animal," were included in Schwartz's first collection, *In Dreams Begin Responsibilities*, for which he received in 1938 his first substantial critical recognition.

In 1939 Laughlin issued Schwartz's translation of Arthur Rimbaud's *Saison en Enfer* (*A Season in Hell*). Schwartz's knowledge of French was imperfect, and in the course of his work he made a number of mistakes. Some of these were misinterpretations of syntactical intricacies in the original, but others were mistranslations of common words. For example, *"troupeaux,"* or "flocks," is rendered as "trumpets"; *"amère"* or "bitter," becomes "stale,"—errors he could have avoided by consulting a dictionary. He also omitted several phrases and sentences from the original, apparently through carelessness. As a result, the translation was received with ferocious disapproval by Justin O'Brien,

Paul Rosenfeld, and Philip Blair Rice, among others. "Justice to all concerned, including Rimbaud," Rice wrote, "would seem to require that it be withdrawn from circulation at once."[12] It was, in fact, withdrawn; but it was reissued in a corrected version the following year.

Despite Schwartz's errors, *A Season in Hell* was even as first published a generally smooth and literate English rendition of Rimbaud. Wallace Stevens defended it against Rice's attack: "Schwartz's translation is considered to be sophomoric. Still, it might be sophomoric from the point of view of translating from one language to another and yet contain things that matter."[13] It has had at least one defender in recent years. Comparing three translations of passages from the original, by Wallace Fowlie, Louise Varèse (whose version New Directions accepted finally), and Schwartz, Roger Shattuck asks, while noting an inaccuracy, "Is it sheer perverseness that makes me find Schwartz's out-of-print version best?"[14]

Shenandoah (1941), an autobiographical play in prose and verse, was eighth in a New Directions series, "The Poet of the Month," which was begun in January, 1941, with William Carlos Williams' collection *The Broken Span* and which continued for several issues. In the same year Schwartz appeared again in the New Directions annual with *Paris and Helen,* a brief play on the Trojan War with a cast of Hollywood actors and actresses. The annual also published "The Isolation of Modern Poetry," which appeared as well in the spring issue of the *Kenyon Review.*

By this time Schwartz was acquiring a reputation as a critic. *Poetry* published in 1936 one of his earliest articles, a review of the poems of Louis MacNeice,[15] and one during the following year on the work of another British poet, Clifford Dyment.[16] "A Note on the Nature of Art" also appeared in 1937 in the *Marxist Quarterly.*[17] The *Southern Review* issued his first major articles in 1938, "Primitivism and Decadence," on Yvor Winters, and "Ernest Hemingway's Literary Situation." Schwartz's work appeared often in this magazine during the next few years, for he contributed articles about Thomas Hardy, William Faulkner, William Butler Yeats, John Dos Passos, and Allen Tate. It is impressive that Schwartz wrote these articles, some of which represent his best critical work, while he was still in his early twenties. In 1938 he also made his first contribution to the

Partisan Review, a critique of Wallace Stevens' *Man with the Blue Guitar.* From then until the mid-1950's he published a great deal of criticism in the magazine, as well as fiction and poetry. Noteworthy among his articles is one on Yeats, published in 1939 shortly after the poet's death, and critiques and reviews of T. S. Eliot, Rainer Maria Rilke, André Gide, Albert Camus, and Saul Bellow, among many others.

Schwartz's career as a poet continued with *Genesis* (1943), a fictional biography in prose and verse that he had begun to write or was planning to write as early as 1931 while a freshman at the University of Wisconsin. Its original title was *Having Snow. Genesis* was to have been three books long; and, according to James Laughlin, it is possible that Schwartz "did write a great deal more of *Genesis,* and then became discouraged about it. . . ."[18]

The World Is a Wedding (1948), assembles the best of his short stories. Wisely, he did not include in this collection either "The Commencement Day Address" or another early story, "An Argument in 1934," a brief study of alienation in New York, which appeared in the *Kenyon Review* in 1942. *Vaudeville for a Princess* (1950), a miscellany of prose and verse, contains some of his least successful poems, and of them he chose to reprint only three in his final collection, *Summer Knowledge* (1959), which was reprinted posthumously as *Selected Poems* in 1967.

In his last book, *Successful Love* (1961), Schwartz collected six later stories that first appeared in the *Avon Book of Modern Writing, Commentary,* the *Kenyon Review,* the *New Yorker,* and the *Partisan Review.* As a group, they show a falling away from the standards of the earlier stories in *The World Is A Wedding,* in which he wrote about his youth, the events and circumstances that shaped his life—a field of strong emotion. The later stories, for the most part, try to depict a wider social milieu that did not concern him so deeply as a writer; and the result is hardly above the level of entertainment. Like a ventriloquist, he tries on a number of voices, as for example in the title story, and abandons the ironic voice of his fictional persona, the grown man looking back upon the obsessive past. Only two of the stories in *Successful Love* seem to deserve special mention here, "The Track Meet" and "The Gift," which have a philosophical and moral intensity that relate them to his earlier work. The collection is not discussed in this study.

Schwartz published little after the beginning of the 1960's. A few poems did appear here and there, notably in the *New Republic*; but there is no record of criticism, with the exception of a foreword to a pamphlet, *Syracuse Poems*, issued by the Department of English of Syracuse University in 1965. The pamphlet consists of poems by five students who were in his class in creative writing. Apparently, Schwartz wrote considerably more than he was ever to publish, including part of a study on T. S. Eliot that was to have been issued by New Directions, but he became discouraged with the project and abandoned it around 1949. Presumably, his magazine articles on Eliot were to have formed part of the book. Friends recall that at one time or another he was considering novels, but it is not at present known how much work was done on these. Some of his literary remains were found in his hotel room after his death, and others were found later in a warehouse. It has been said that they are all in the possession of his literary executor and friend of long standing, Dwight Macdonald.

Selected Essays of Delmore Schwartz, a collection of fifty-five articles and reviews edited by two of his colleagues at Syracuse University, was published posthumously in 1970 by the University of Chicago Press; and this publication realized a project that Schwartz himself had contemplated.

CHAPTER 2

Isolation and Vocation

I *"The Journey to the Foreign Country"*

S CHWARTZ came of age in a decade that saw the emergence of a generation of new writers that included Robert Lowell, Randall Jarrell, Isaac Rosenfeld, Karl Shapiro, John Berryman, Saul Bellow, and Muriel Rukeyser, all of whom were born around the time of World War I. Specifically, Schwartz belongs to a group of Jewish American writers whose achievement was to bring their experience as Jews into the mainstream of American writing.

The 1930's was a time when writers in one way or another had to come to terms with the conditions brought about by the Depression. As Schwartz himself observed later, "All modern writing was judged by one criterion: its relationship to the social and economic crises."[1] Much of his own work is related to these "crises" in that it faithfully reflects his reactions to the Depression and its effects, immediate and intimate, upon family, social, and personal life. However, he does not appear to have been actively committed to the radical doctrines that were so popular among intellectuals during the decade. Although he expounded Marxist theory in some of his writing, it was primarily for the artistic purpose of providing one of a number of intellectual vantage points from which to interpret and formulate experience. His work, though charged—sometimes ridden—with ideas, is not didactic.

By the 1930's British and American poets had achieved successes that collectively signified the triumph of modern poetry in English. With that triumph came a flowering of critical theory and exegesis—an inventory, in large part—of the gains of the previous decades, to which poets themselves, such as Allen Tate, John Crowe Ransom, and R. P. Blackmur, made notable contri-

24

butions. Schwartz belongs among them as a poet who was articulate about the craft of poetry. He was influenced by several of his older and more famous contemporaries, and as a critic he wrote perceptively about their work.

T. S. Eliot, the "literary dictator" of England and America, as Schwartz called him, was then at the height of his fame. Eliot engrossed Schwartz more than any other modern poet. Although he was not blindly uncritical of Eliot's dictatorial role or of some of his poetry—he was dubious about the value of some of his later plays and *Four Quartets*—he did, for the most part, admire him. He also tended to identify himself with Eliot, so much so that what he says about him reveals what he thought his own role in particular and that of poets in general to be in the modern world.

In the first of three published articles about Eliot, Schwartz calls him a "culture hero." The culture hero, he says, must be an innovator; he develops new forms and a new idiom that will make it possible to express hitherto unrealizable approaches to reality. "Some make the vehicles by means of which a mountain is climbed, some may climb the mountain, and some apprehend the new view. . . . T. S. Eliot is a culture hero in each of these three ways." Furthermore, Eliot is the poet of modern life: "The width and the height and the depths of modern life are exhibited in his poetry; the agony and the horror of modern life are represented as inevitable to any human being who does not wish to deceive himself with systematic lies." More specifically, Eliot is an "international hero." His family background and his migration to England from St. Louis make him "the descendant of the essential characters of James."[2]

He is also an international hero because of his historical awareness. Like the seer Tiresias in *The Waste Land*, Eliot sees the moment in time in its historical perspective. An international hero is possible because "we have become an international people. . . . Just as the war [World War II, still being fought at the date of this article] is international, so the true causes of many of the things in our lives are world-wide, and we are able to understand the character of our lives only when we are aware of all history. . . ."[3]

Historical awareness is necessary for understanding the modern predicament. Eliot is modern in his approach to the theme

of love, which "often, in modern life ... has been the worst sick-
ness of human beings."[4] In Eliot's poetry, love, as distinguished
from copulation, is despaired of, and the failure to love is a
symptom of a modern disease. "Difficulty in love is inseparable
from the deracination from which the international man suffers."
When love becomes "purely personal," when it loses its com-
munal being because of the failure of traditional values and
institutions, then it "does become merely copulation."[5]

Some of these claims for Eliot are excessive and overemotional.
To be aware of "all history," for example, was not in Eliot's
power, as it seems to be implied, and it is hardly in the power of
any man. Discussion of Schwartz's work will show how obsessed
he was by history, often to the detriment of his poetry, and how
the failure to love, with its counterpart, a longing for love, is a
constant preoccupation.

It may seem strange, at first thought, that the son of Jewish
immigrants should choose as a model a poet who was noted for
his political conservatism and his Anglo-Catholic sympathies and
who on occasion was capable of anti-Semitic remarks and references. Schwartz was, in fact, disturbed by these traces of anti-
Semitism, but Eliot as the epitome of the poet-intellectual remained for Schwartz an object worthy of respect and emulation.[6]
Also, Eliot considered as an exile, a lonely witness to "the agony
and the horror of modern life," might have appealed to Schwartz
in part precisely because of his own Jewishness.

Concluding his article, Schwartz says that "modern life may
be compared to a foreign country in which a foreign language
is spoken." Eliot "has made the journey to the foreign country
and described the nature of the new life in the foreign country."[7]
In "The Isolation of Modern Poetry," Schwartz outlines the
reasons why the poet is alienated in modern life. His argument
seems familiar enough in some instances, but it is worthwhile
to present it here in a paraphrase with quotations, for it lies
at the heart of his concern as a practicing poet, and leads to a
discussion of the conditions that influenced his style, especially
that of his prose.

The poet, he says, "has been separated from the whole life
of society," and as a result modern poetry is obscure. The
process of separation began with "the gradual destruction of
the world picture which ... had for a long time been taken for

granted by the poet." This "world picture" was that of the Bible (he might have referred to medieval cosmology as well), which had "provided a view of the universe which circumscribed the area in which anyone ventured to think or use his imagination." It would be a mistake to believe that "this view of the universe had not been disturbed in numerous ways long before the modern poet arrived upon the scene." Still, no poet before Blake experienced the conflict "between two pictures of the world, the picture provided by the Bible and the one provided by the physical sciences."[8]

In the nineteenth century, however, "the conflict became so radical and so obvious that no poet of ambition can seriously avoid it." The explanations of science were not harmful to the poet because they pictured an overwhelmingly large universe. Theologians and philosophers "know that size is not a particularly important aspect of anything; but the poet must *see*, and what he has had to see was this incongruity between the importance man attributes to himself and his smallness against the background of the physical world of 19th century science."[9]

With the coming of the industrial age, the poet also suffered a cultural displacement: "There was no room in the increasing industrialization of society for such a monster as the cultivated man." As a result, "it became increasingly impossible for the poet to write about the lives of other men; for not only was he removed from their lives, but, above all, the culture and the sensibility which made him a poet could not be employed when the proposed subject was the lives of human beings in whom culture and sensibility had no organic function."[10]

This last remark is open to question. "Culture" and "sensibility," while some poets may possess both to an extraordinary degree, may not be so rare as Schwartz imagines, despite the fact that an appreciation of poetry—and poetry of *any* time—is rare enough. Nor does there seem to be any reason why the poet may not take as his subject "the lives of human beings" who are without culture in the exclusive sense of the word. That he may is amply demonstrated by such widely different writers as Edgar Lee Masters, with his *Spoon River Anthology*, Edward Arlington Robinson, and, more recently, William Carlos Williams, who portrays ordinary life with tremendous delicacy and insight. In fact, Schwartz himself betrays his own statement; for some of his best short stories are about people who have little culture and no poetic sensibility. It is true, however, that the modern poet hardly has an audience among them.

The poet in his cultural isolation, Schwartz continues, must struggle to find an effective personal idiom. "The trouble has been that the idiom of poetic style and the normal thought and speech of the community have been moving in opposite directions and have little or no relationship to each other." Precisely because "the private life of his sensibility is the chief subject available to [the poet], it becomes increasingly necessary to have recourse to new and special uses of language."[11] Such recourse would seem to be necessary also when the subject is other than his own sensibility. Or it may be more accurate to say that the cultural and linguistic isolation of the modern poet compels a greater degree of self-reflection than that experienced by writers in an established tradition, a greater concentration upon his personal idiom and his own relationship to the subject, whatever that may be.

All too simply, Schwartz concludes that for the modern poet "the common language" is "the opposite of what he needs."[12] The article does not consider the ways whereby modern poets have used ordinary language for artistic ends. Elsewhere, however, as in another of his articles on Eliot, "T. S. Eliot's Voice and His Voices," Schwartz discusses the subject in some detail, observing that there has been in modern poetry generally "an effort to assimilate the everyday world, the modern world, and colloquial speech by the use of everyday and prosaic words."[13]

In "The Vocation of the Poet in the Modern World" he says that even the misuse of language in ordinary speech can be fruitful for the poet. Of course, he "must resist the innumerable ways in which words are spoiled, misused, commercialized, deformed, mispronounced, and in general degraded." Still, "the disease which degrades language in the modern world helps bring about the remarkable and often multilingual sensitivity of the modern poet to the language which is the matrix from which he draws his poems."[14]

Schwartz believes that the reason "language is misused, whether fruitfully or not, is that in modern life experience has become international."[15] Immigration and travel, for example, create new language situations. He thus returns to the international theme, and he describes Joyce, as well as Eliot, as being an "international hero." Joyce exemplifies this role in his use of language: "All that has been observed in Eliot's work is all the more the case with *Finnegan's Wake*—the attention to colloquial speech, the awareness of the variety of ways in which language can be degraded, and how that degradation can be the base for new originality and exactitude, the sense of being involved and affected by all history."[16] The essential thesis of "The Isolation of Modern Poetry"—that the poet is divided from the modern world and must devise his own idiom—is not refuted but qualified. The poet has a sensitive ear that overhears the nuances of modern speech, which may take on a heightened value in his work, becoming a concrete representation of the tone and temper of modern life.

Schwartz's observations are reflected in his own writing, especially in the major stories of *The World Is a Wedding*, where he frequently employs a deliberately simple, flat, and banal style that mirrors the quality of the life observed and the speech, values, and mentality of his characters. He often pretends to be as artless as they are, as ignorant of the literary graces. This style picks up and incorporates numerous colloquialisms, clichés, and errors which receive an ironic emphasis by the mere fact of having been overheard and set down by an effaced and impersonal narrator. Schwartz is speaking about his own method when he describes the implicitly ironic approach of Ring Lardner to his own world: "In a short story by Ring Lardner . . . the irony of the writer . . . is never expressed through any character, or any explicit judgment, but it is there sometimes in the form of a grammatical error and pun, such as 'the world serious,' sometimes in a brief exaggeration of tone."[17]

The writer's sense of being an outsider in modern society, of occupying a position apart, conduces to another stylistic strain: the parody of literary or educated language. This characteristic often appears in Schwartz's stories together with his play on ordinary speech. In the brief, anecdotal story "A Bitter Farce," from *The World Is a Wedding*, he coins the term "mock-grand" to describe the consciously absurd, deliberately pompous use of such language by his fictional self, Shenandoah Fish—the name itself epitomizes the grandiose linked with the banal—before a class of ignorant young students. The same expression

appears in an article about John Crowe Ransom and Wallace
Stevens, published about the same time as the story: "Both poets
make a like use of dandyism of surface, of irony, and of a mock-
grand style."[18] One reason for their doing so is that "when the
poet is regarded as a strange, rare, and abnormal being, it is
natural that he should mock at the same time as he enjoys the
language of the grand manner."[19] For the most part, Schwartz's
fictional style is that of a man who sees through and around
everything; who, furthermore, is detached and ironic even in
respect to himself. Often the very act of consciousness has an
inflection of self-mockery.

The poet or writer also has difficulty in the twentieth century
in finding ways to inform his work with ideas, beliefs, and values.
"Everyone has not only his own point of view," Schwartz says
in his preface to *Genesis,* "but his own view of Life. No author
can assume a community of ideas and values between himself
and his audience."[20] As a speculative and philosophical poet,
Schwartz often considers this problem in his criticism, most
notably in "Poetry and Belief in Thomas Hardy," which is
discussed with *Genesis.* At present, it suffices to remark that
Schwartz felt that the purpose of ideas, beliefs, and values in
poetry, apart from whatever validity they may have in themselves as statements of truth, is to give shape to the writer's
experience. Thus, in an article about R. P. Blackmur, he says
that "beliefs in most poetry are only a means, a framework to
help the poet represent the ragged, unwieldy facts of experience."[21] And in a review of books by Albert Camus he declares: "The truth or falsity of an author's ideas are less important than the fact that his ideas make possible a grasp of
experience and the composition of first-rate literary works."[22]

II   *"Alienated and Indestructible"*

Schwartz's sense of being isolated in the modern world as a
poet was heightened by his awareness of his Jewish heritage,
one which throughout most of Western history has entailed
varying degrees of estrangement from the main body of society.
Joyce, Schwartz observes toward the conclusion of "The Vocation of the Poet in the Modern World," was aware of a similarity
between the poet and the Jew, and for this reason he "identi-

fied himself with Jews, with Leopold Bloom, an Irish Jew, and with the character of Shem in his last book. . . ." For the sake of his vocation, the poet must be prepared to suffer and endure like the Jews themselves. The Jew, he says, "is at once alienated and indestructible, he is an exile from his own country, exiled from himself, yet he survives the annihilating fury of history. In the unpredictable and fearful future that awaits civilization, the poet must be prepared to be alienated and indestructible."[23]

However, though the Jew stands apart in his alienation, he also epitomizes a common predicament; for in the modern world alienation is universal—a premise that seems to underlie much contemporary Jewish American writing, and one that Schwartz, by the evidence of his own words and practice, accepted as being true. In Schwartz's short stories about New York Jewish life, his study of alienation includes not only disaffected poets and intellectuals but people from customary walks of life. Because of the poet's special position, he may suffer more from isolation; but he does not suffer alone.

Schwartz described his Jewish background and its influence upon his work in a symposium of young Jewish writers published in 1944. His upbringing, he says, did not make him particularly aware of his Jewish identity, and anti-Semitism was "merely something heard about." It was "an interesting abstraction, or . . . part of the barbarous past." If there was contempt of any kind, it was "the easy contempt for all kinds of immigrants which dominates the national humor."[24] He regards his experience as typical of the years from 1920 to 1933 in New York before Hitler came into power in Germany. Inherited tradition had little place in Schwartz's childhood; but despite his ignorance, "the fact of Jewishness was a matter of naïve and innocent pride, untouched by any sense of fear."[25]

Passages of *Genesis,* assuming they are autobiographical, seem to belie his statement that he was unaware of anti-Semitism as a child. However, in the present article he says that he was sheltered from it until he went to school outside of New York. When he first encountered it, he imagined that he was disliked for faults in his own character. He remarks wryly that he was protected because he had always felt left out, even by Jews. It was the "revival of political anti-Semitism" that finally made him aware of "the difference between being left out by Christians and by Jews." He began to comprehend "the social anti-Semitism which had always been part of my experience without my understanding that it was certainly present."[26] A manifesto follows:

All of this ignorance and growing recognition has been important to me as an author. . . . My ignorance, my weakness of being too personal, my self-concern—each of these traits in itself an evil—helped me to regard my own experience with other human beings as a common and universal thing, and not local or regional or racial. . . . And then, when I knew enough to distinguish between the different kinds of alienation, this knowledge illuminated my own mind for me in the most fruitful way. . . . I understood my own personal squint at experience; and the fact of being a Jew became available to me as a central symbol of alienation, bias, point of view, and certain other characteristics which are the peculiar marks of modern life, and as I think now, the essential ones. And thus I have to say . . . that the fact of Jewishness has been nothing but an ever-growing good to me, and it seems clear to me now that it can be, at least for me, nothing but a fruitful and inexhaustible inheritance.[27]

One short story, "A Bitter Farce," deals exclusively with certain basic antagonisms between Jews and gentiles. Shenandoah Fish must confront the anti-Semitism of his students, which they not only reveal in their deliberated opinions but also betray in their unthinking choice of words. Shenandoah's point of view is so close to that of the poet himself that Schwartz seems to be speaking in his own voice as his hero tells the class:

I feel very proud of my ancestors, who wrote the Bible and other great works of aspiration, morality and fiction which have been the basis of Western culture for the past two thousand years at least. My ancestors, in whom I take pride, but not personal pride, were scholars, poets, prophets and students of God when most of Europe worshipped sticks and stones; not that I hold that against any of you, for it is not your fault if your forebears were barbarians grovelling and groping about for peat or something.[28]

This encounter gives rise to "innumerable anxiety feelings which had their source in events which had occurred for the past five thousand years."[29]

Schwartz came of age just when the Jewish American writer

was becoming conscious of himself and his place in American society and when aspects of Jewish American life were acquiring a universal quality and appeal. In contrast to that time, the present witnesses a popularization of Jewish themes that has resulted in travesties of Jewish family life. Leslie Fiedler says that the Jewish writer achieved success just when "the popular acceptance of his alienation as a satisfactory symbol for the human condition threatens to turn it into an affectation, a fashionable cliché."[30] Schwartz's fiction, however, is unsentimental and uncompromising.

Alienation in Schwartz's work is first of all the deracination of immigrant families in America. The children of these families, for the most part frustrated writers and intellectuals, suffer most; but an unvoiced, unrealized loneliness pervades the lives of most of his characters. Confronted by a world that does not answer to their ideals and desires, the members of the younger generation experience a loss of purpose, a weakening of their sense of self-identity and the reality of others.

There is another form of alienation, which Schwartz seems to have regarded as absolute, a part of the human condition—namely, that the self lives in essential isolation from other selves. In his earlier work, Schwartz despairs of the possibility of real communion between people; for he believes that one can see oneself only subjectively, and others only as objects; one cannot grant that others are as real as oneself, or, on the other hand, realize that one is an object in the eyes of others, limited and relative—in time, above all.

It is possible that Schwartz's Jewishness made him especially sensitive to time, a dominant presence in his work. Certainly, his interest in history has a specifically Jewish orientation, as in *Genesis*, where many of the characters have Old Testament names, and where family history recapitulates, with its trials and migrations, the history of the Jewish people. Concern with the Jewish past opens upon an interest in history on a larger scale and in archetypal events and characters that give a universal dimension to the life of the hero.

Finally, it should be noted that Schwartz's ironic style, which reflects his general sense of alienation, was affected by the immigrant background of his family. "To an author, and especially to a poet," he writes, such a background "may give a heightened sensitivity to language, a sense of idiom, and a sense of how much expresses itself through colloquialism. But it also produces in some a fear of mispronunciation; a hesitation in speech; and a sharpened focus upon the characters of his parents. And in some, especially if they are interested in teaching literature, the cultivation of a fantastic precision of speech and an accent which is more English than the English accent...."[31]

The English of Schwartz's intellectual characters, who are mostly children of immigrants and have values that set them apart from their parents and from American life in general, is extremely cultivated for the most part—at times to the point of absurdity. They are aware of this comic strain and at times slip into "mock-grand" self-parody. They also have "a sense of how much expresses itself through colloquialism," and so they in turn mock the idioms of ordinary speech. One has the impression that they and the author himself are standing a bit to the side of the English language, just as they are standing a bit to the side of life.

CHAPTER 3

In the Mirror of Art

MUCH of Schwartz's early work reflects the circumstances and background of his own life. It is informed by an attitude toward experience that might be called ironic hyper-consciousness, and it arises in part from his awareness of his anomalous position as a poet and intellectual in modern society. Consciousness stands in opposition to experience and to the everyday world that has little awareness of itself. Heinz Politzer has succinctly defined an important aspect of this polarity:

There is the world of his own experience, as constituted by his biography, memories, and immediate feelings. This he has fixed in time and called childhood; he has also fixed it in space, in Brooklyn. . . . Beyond this sphere of real life, there lies the world of his education, full of the names of books, famous men, and images taken from books: an abstract universe of intelligence where he developed his consciousness. . . . The incompatibility of experience and consciousness—the contradiction between the banality and ugliness of daily life and the truth and beauty of intellectual existence—has remained ever present to Schwartz.[1]

Consciousness and experience resist reconciliation. The hyper-conscious observer of life is characteristically a figure of futility, incapable of influencing the world he surveys. He is always incapable, of course, when he surveys it from a point of removal in time. Moreover, the problem that men are subjects to themselves, objects to others, resists solution. To give formal expression to these points of view, Schwartz often sets up a relationship between a scene of action, usually in the past, and an observer or group of observers who try to encompass an event with their futile and ironic consciousness. His forms and metaphors are essentially theatrical. The typical observer—or witness

35

—is at once detached from and involved in the action he beholds. Particular facts are often given a universal relevance by means of philosophical exegesis and citations from many areas of cultural reference, such as history, myth, and literature.

I *"He Is a Person"*

The central characters of much of Schwartz's work are fictional representations of himself, such as Shenandoah Fish in the play *Shenandoah* and some of the stories, and Hershey Green, the hero of *Genesis*. Less obviously, aspects of the author appear in characters that are not directly or deliberately autobiographical, as, for example, intellectual characters like Jacob and Rudyard in "The World Is a Wedding." It is also likely that Samuel and Jasper in "The Child Is the Meaning of This Life" reveal contradictory facets of Schwartz's personality.

Schwartz belongs among those writers whose work, while undergoing the transforming and universalizing process of art, derives directly from their personal experience. Often his writing is a mirror in which he sees chiefly himself; in fact, the mirror recurs in his work as a symbol of self-scrutiny, and he frequently refers to Narcissus. There is a narcissistic side to his characters which he recognizes and explicitly develops.[2]

Selfhood—the nature and the mystery of the self—is Schwartz's chief concern and the center of his philosophical speculations. For example, both *Genesis* and *Shenandoah* consider the hero in relation to the forces that have determined his being and his character and meditate upon the possibility of individual freedom in the face of chance and necessity. In *Coriolanus and His Mother,* the hero in his dilemma of having to choose between Rome and allegiance to its enemy the Volscians represents the self at the point of junction of the past and the future; he is determined by the first and yet somehow free to choose his own way and make his own world in the time to come.

"And he moves, because he must," Schwartz writes in his prose introduction to Act 5, "He Is a Person"; "and thus he is betrayed to the unending agony of conscious being. . . . He must create what has never existed. . . . He is the future. He is a person! . . . His freedom creates the future. He is the mystery, irreducible. His freedom is his mystery. . . . With that mystery, his own identity, he . . . invents the future! . . . Coriolanus, the individual."[3]

Uniqueness, freedom, and the future are equated. Every moment offers the possibility of choice, and the individual is perpetually responsible for creating his own self by choosing. This point of view, which is decidedly existentialist, represents one aspect of Schwartz's concern with beginnings out of the past in the direction of the unknown future. Birth itself, or genesis, to refer to the title of his longest work, is the primary beginning. In the story "In Dreams Begin Responsibilities," he also dramatizes the beginning of manhood, after a dream of the past; and many of his later poems in *Summer Knowledge* (or *Selected Poems*) describe a spiritual rebirth.

II *The Fire of Time and the Agony of Conscious Being*

Coriolanus is "betrayed to the unending agony of conscious being." The discipline of extreme consciousness, which calls for relentless self-examination and the resurrection of the past by memory, is a means for getting a hold on the flux of life and for establishing one's identity. The enemy of the self is time, and to relax one's self-awareness is to surrender to time. "Calmly We Walk through This April's Day," an early poem, ends with the prayerlike wish:

> May memory restore again and again
> The smallest color of the smallest day:
> Time is the school in which we learn,
> Time is the fire in which we burn.[4]

Memory is supposed to be redemptive, and presumably the purpose of "conscious being" is to lead to action that will create the future. Yet, at the heart of this emphasis on consciousness is a paradox: while considered a positive good, a means of integrating the self, consciousness becomes an end in itself for Schwartz's incredibly self-absorbed and retrospective heroes, a substitute for living and acting. Their self-enforced isolation from life is a condition for knowing, which in turn can only widen the rift between themselves and the world.

Is consciousness a blessing or a curse? The past cannot be changed; and on the other hand, action in the present is impossible. The all-wise and all-passive ghosts that haunt Schwartz's work exemplify the plight of the living. Furthermore, life cannot be known at the moment that it is lived. Knowledge must of necessity be too late. The perspective upon the past receives an ironic emphasis in that the observer is characteristically so strongly attached to the past scene that he often forgets his distance in time and tries to change what is beyond reach. *Shenandoah* and "In Dreams Begin Responsibilities" dramatize the irony inherent in this hopeless situation.

With their futile intelligence, many of Schwartz's characters seem to be hardly more than the ghosts of their own selves, haunting their own lives. Dwelling largely upon the past and not upon the supposedly free future, they become obsessed by the fatality of things, by deterministic forces. The irrevocable past has not only determined the present, but it will also repeat itself in the future. History, whether personal or universal, is cyclical: the past is reborn, the child is foredoomed to commit the sins and make the mistakes of the father; and human history itself, as Schwartz says at the close of "In the Naked Bed, in Plato's Cave," is "unforgiven."

Images of circularity, repetition, and the like appear throughout Schwartz's earlier works to describe the world and the self bound in time and history. Just as the claims of consciousness are challenged by the view that it is futile, so the putative freedom of the individual to act, to change, to make the future, is challenged by the view that the forces of the past and necessity are inescapable.

III   *Blue Sky, White Snow: Images of Transcendence*

Throughout his work Schwartz depicts an imagined spiritual reality that stands in contrast to the banal, everyday world and existence in time. In his earlier work, some of his ideas and references have a Platonic cast; or he may portray God as the supreme spectator of the world, as in *Genesis*; or as intelligence absolute, in which the doctor of *Dr. Bergen's Belief* places his faith, maintaining that strict and scrupulous attempts to be as conscious as possible emulate the transcendent consciousness of the deity. The mediator here between God and man is the blue sky, the eye of God.

The blue sky is a thematic image in other works, such as *Genesis* and some of the poems, early and late. In "Socrates' Ghost Must Haunt Me Now" the philosopher

> . . . stands by me stockstill,
> Teaching hope to my flickering will,
> Pointing to the sky's inexorable blue
> —Old Noumenon, come true, come true!

Representing a reality that lies beyond sense experience, beyond the phenomenal world, Socrates tells the poet that "the mechanical whims of appetite" are all that he has "of conscious choice" and that "the butterfly caged in electric light/ Is my only day in the world's great night. . . ." Although he intends to teach hope, the tone of the poem is exasperated if not despairing; for the blue sky is "inexorable," not moved by prayers, beyond reach.[5]

Two other images appear as symbols of a higher world, beyond "the mechanical whims of appetite": starlight and snow. The first, like the sky itself, has associations with superior or transcendent consciousness. One of the ghosts that appear as commentators in *Genesis* says, " 'Here at the heights at least our thoughts are free,/ Like the grave starlight far above a storm—' "[6] In "Prothalamion," "The perfect stars persist/ Small in the guilty night. . . ."[7] The image receives its fullest development in "Starlight Like Intuition Pierced the Twelve," a later poem.

Snow, as Alfred Kazin notes, "recurs through all of Delmore's work as the symbol of joy, of the other world for which he longed more than he did for anything else."[8] It appears as such at the end of "In Dreams Begin Responsibilities," in "A Dog Named Ego, the Snowflakes as Kisses," in "New Year's Eve," and in many other places as well. It is also the subject of "The Statues," a parable in the tradition of Franz Kafka, in which a miraculous and prolonged snowfall upon New York covers the ground with marvelous statues that arouse wonder and delight, bringing people together and causing metaphysical speculation as to their nature and origin. Some think of them as a metaphor for "the way that the haunted and hunted lives of human beings took shape by an unpredictable and continuous fall to which little or no designing agency could be attributed."[9] Faber Gottschalk, the story's only identifiable character, addresses a crowd: ". . . must we not . . . regard them as sacred mysteries, at least for the time being? Who knows what relationship they may not have to our lives? What natural or supernatural powers may

not, through them, be signing to us?" Soon after, "a tireless and
foul rain" washes them away; and the city returns to its violence
and disorder.[10]

The original title of *Genesis* was *Having Snow*, and in it the
image appears most frequently. Watching a snowfall, the young
hero Hershey feels "Hallucinatory calm, utter quiet pleasure
(as falling towards the depths of sleep, the grateful coma)...."
The snow is "The death of the colored world, the final fineness
of Nature."[11] It suggests a loss of consciousness deeply desired
by the self-obsessed hero. It stands for oblivion, and, by extension, annihilation and death.

The loss is not entirely privative, however. Earlier this bliss
is likened to that of the souls of the dead in Heaven who, " 'risen
at last/ to full eternity,' " gaze upon " 'The infinite light that makes
the universe,/ And know a pleasure perfect and serene!' "[12] The
metaphor suggests that there is a necessary connection between
death and transcendence: the bliss of heaven can be attained
only through death. On the other hand, Heaven is "infinite light."
It is at once the abode of those who have died to this world and
the creative source of this world. Snow, which underlies the
metaphor through comparison with light, represents both beginnings and ends, both life and death, both the extinction of
consciousness and a transcendent awareness "perfect and serene."

What above all gives snow its symbolic power to embrace
these extremes is its whiteness. White is both the absence of
color, as such suggesting annihilation and death, and the color
of light, which is the source of all color. The whiteness of light
is the whiteness of a pure potential that generates all of the
colorful variety of the visual world, just as the sun, the source
of light itself, generates all life. With its wintry whiteness, snow
stands for death and absence; but, on the other hand, through
its association with light, it may also stand for life, joy, hope,
and transcendence, for miraculous beginnings and sources.

In Schwartz's later poems light replaces snow as the dominant
image, becoming the central symbol of his "summer knowledge."
The change is anticipated in *Genesis* itself as the poet passes
directly from his description of the snow as the "death of the
colored world" to a hymn to the light as the "source of all the
forces."[13] The association of the two images becomes explicit
in a poem from his final collection, "The First Morning of the

Second World," in which he imagines a metamorphosis of falling snow into light. This change represents what might be called the acclimation of the transcendent to the earth, to "The kingdom of heaven on earth on Sunday summer day," [*sic*] as he says in his poem on a light-filled painting by Georges Seurat.[14] Similarly, the blue sky undergoes a metamorphosis, notably in the same poem, where its blueness becomes that of the river which reflects it, bringing it to earth as it were.

IV   *"Let Us Consider Where the Great Men Are"*

The world of culture, which is on the side of consciousness, stands in opposition to the world of experience. The saints and guardians of that higher world are the great artists and savants to whom Schwartz again and again pays homage. In *Shenandoah*, the hero as a grown-up commentator on the play, in which he appears as a baby about to be named and circumcised, invokes the great writers—among them Joyce, Eliot, Yeats, Kafka, and Rilke—who at that moment in the past were living and working far from the Brooklyn living room of his infancy. "Let us consider where the great men are," he begins, "Who will obsess this child when he can read." These writers are exiles in a world they cannot change. Their glory is in their bearing witness:

> All over Europe these exiles find in art
> What exile is: art becomes exile too,
> A secret and a code studied in secret,
> Declaring the agony of modern life:
> This child will learn of life from these great men,
> He will participate in their solitude. . . .[15]

The great men that appear in Schwartz's work are dead, or else they are seen, as here, at some moment in the past. Death or remoteness in time endows them with a heroic, a legendary aspect. Together, they represent the poet's spiritual ancestry. Like many modern writers, Schwartz turns to a certified greatness in the past for solace, identity, and justification in the face of self-doubt and loneliness in the present. He resembles Baudelaire especially, the prototype of the modern poet, "the stranger," as Schwartz calls him in "The Isolation of Modern Poetry," after the title of one of Baudelaire's own poems.[16]

For Baudelaire, as for Schwartz, art had a spiritually redemptive, almost a religious function. In "Les Phares" ("The Lighthouses"), God Himself is called upon to witness the greatness of the painters whom the poem celebrates. According to Jean-Paul Sartre, it is a "census" of Baudelaire's "spiritual order."[17] The poet admired Edgar Allan Poe most of all, for in Poe's life he saw a reflection of his own fate and its justification. Sartre's remarks about what he considers to be the primary cause of this admiration are relevant to Schwartz's own adulation of the great, and it is interesting that Sartre and Schwartz use an almost identical image to describe Baudelaire's psychological relationship to Poe.

Sartre believes that the "identity of fate" that Baudelaire felt joined him to the American poet

> . . . only interested him *because Poe was dead.* If he had been alive, [Poe] would have been no more than a vague body like his own. . . . Once he was dead, however, his portrait assumed its final form and its features became clear. It was perfectly natural to describe him as a poet and martyr; his existence had become a destiny. . . . It was then that the resemblances acquired their full value; they transformed Poe . . . into an image in Baudelaire's past. . . . Baudelaire leant over the depths of the years . . . and suddenly he caught sight of his own reflection in the gray waters of the past. That's what he *is.* At once his existence was consecrated.[18]

In "The Masters of the Heart Touched the Unknown," from Schwartz's *Vaudeville for a Princess,* a poem on writers that somewhat resembles "Les Phares," the French poet is portrayed in the same brooding posture: "Baudelaire slumped in deadly tiredness/ And saw his own face in the tragic play/ Of Poe's face which like drowned Ophelia lay."[19] The water (implied by "drowned Ophelia") is a mirror; "the tragic play" is both a play of the features and a drama. The comparison shows the similarity between the mirror, a symbol for introspection in Schwartz's work, and the plays, or playlike situations, in which much of his work is cast, where the hero, who represents the writer to begin with, observes either himself at some other stage of his life or a scene that intimately concerns him. To a degree, worship of the great is another form of self-contemplation, and has a narcissistic aspect.

V "The Capital of Departure"

The City of New York, Schwartz's familiar locale, appears in his work as a place of abomination, the very opposite of the desired world, the sublimated world of culture presided over by "the great men"; yet it was the ground of his existence. Schwartz seldom describes it; but he often refers to the city, sometimes ironically. To Jacob Cohen, the main character of "The World Is a Wedding," it is "the capital of departure," a city that offers every luxury to those who have money and, when luxuries pall, offers easy means of escape. But for Jacob and his friends, impoverished by the Depression, it is the place "in which they lived and were lost." As "the capital of departure," New York offers no true community; it fulfills no traditional function. In its immensity, with its vast number of inhabitants, the city is unassimilable. As Jacob ruminates, "No human being can take in such an aggregation: all that we know is that there is always more and more. This is the moreness of which we are aware, no matter what we look upon. This moreness is the true being of the great city, so that, in a way, this city hardly exists. It certainly does not exist as does our family, our friends, and our neighborhood."[20]

Jacob's attitude prevails in Schwartz's fiction, in which the focus of attention is family, friends, and the apartments in which they live. Nevertheless, beyond these enclaves one senses the impersonal city as a force that shuts in and weighs down upon the characters. New York has an atmospheric rather than a physical presence, and its impersonality is heightened by the very absence of concrete detail in his stories. Images of the metropolis appear, however, in some of Schwartz's poems, in which they symbolize the inescapable reality that opposes the imagination, idealism, and transcendence that compose the other half of the poet's world. The idea of the city as the antagonist of hope and desire is most completely embodied in three early poems, "Someone Is Harshly Coughing as Before," "Tired and Unhappy, You Think of Houses," and the sonnet, "O City, City."

The first of these is a picture of isolation in "the great city" on the eve of World War II.[21] The narrator of the poem listens to an unknown neighbor "harshly coughing on the next floor." Dismissing the idea of going to help him, he proceeds

from this minimum of detail to identify the stranger as "God,
who has caught a cold again,/ Wandering helplessly in the
world once more. . . ." He is also "poor Keats," genius early dead,
"longing for Eden, afraid of the coming war." The following
strophe of this poem describes the city as seen through a window
at dusk. It becomes a metaphor for the actual world, the world
turning in the endless cycle of time, the opposite of Eden, the
imagined world:

> The past, a giant shadow like the twilight,
> The moving street on which the autos slide,
> The buildings' heights, like broken teeth,
> Repeat necessity on every side,
> The age requires a death and is not denied,
> He has come as a young man to be hanged once more!

Whether one thinks of the neighbor as Christ or Keats, he is
the Victim who appears again and again throughout time. History, "the past," is identified with the approaching shadow of
night and with the mechanical movement of the earth. With its
buildings and traffic, the metropolis is the image of the impersonal and relentless forces that oppose the visionary Eden.

In "Tired and Unhappy, You Think of Houses,"[22] the reality
of the city is contrasted with a dream of private happiness in
surroundings of wealth and ease—in "houses/ Soft-carpeted and
warm in the December evening. . . ." In one of these, "a young
girl" sings the aria from Gluck's *Orpheus and Eurydice* in which
"Orpheus pleads with Death" to restore his dead wife to the
living world. As she sings, "Her elders watch, nodding their
happiness/ To see time fresh again in her self-conscious eyes. . . ."
The girl's self-consciousness may suggest that the dream itself
is graceless and specious. Returning to reality, the dreamer
finds himself "Where the underground is charged, where the
weight/ Of the lean buildings is seen. . . ." He is actually in
the subway, an "underground" which recalls Hades, the setting
of the myth. By implication, the subway and the city itself
signify spiritual death. Surrounded by the "anonymous" crowd,
the dreamer is "caught in an anger exact as a machine!"

"O City, City,"[23] expresses most completely the antithesis
between the mechanical, death-ridden city and the dream of love
and life—a dream that seems as destined to fail as Orpheus'

attempt to rescue Eurydice. Again the subway is associated with death, here present in "his loud picture," perhaps a reference to garish advertisements as manifestations of spiritual emptiness. Yet, if the picture is "loud," the citizens of New York, "six million souls," are silent, "their breath/ An empty song suppressed on every side. . . ." Death is also in the traffic, in "the sliding auto's catastrophe," and in "the office building" that "rises to its tyranny." To live here is "our anguished diminution until we die."

This portrayal of spiritual anguish occupies the octet of the sonnet, while the sestet beautifully provides the antithesis:

> Whence, if ever, shall come the actuality
> Of a voice speaking the mind's knowing,
> The sunlight bright on the green windowshade,
> And the self articulate, affectionate, and flowing,
> Ease, warmth, light, the utter showing,
> When in the white bed all things are made.

The whiteness of the bed, place of love and place of genesis, recalls both the purity of the snow and the glory of the light "bright on the green windowshade." The sestet is a question that echoes longingly throughout Schwartz's work.

CHAPTER 4

In Dreams Begin Responsibilities:
The Lyrics

IN DREAMS BEGIN RESPONSIBILITIES (1938) represents the full scope of Schwartz's interests and obsessions; and it prefigures all of his work to come. He ranges in form from the short lyric to the long poem, from play to short story. A book of attack, it is intellectually ambitious and poetically experimental. Although it has long been out of print, its contents are available in various later collections, with the exception of the play, *Dr. Bergen's Belief.* The title story appeared in *The World Is a Wedding* and has been widely anthologized. The long poem *Coriolanus and His Mother* was reprinted in *Summer Knowledge* (or *Selected Poems*), as were all of the lyrics, many of which were first published in the *Partisan Review, Poetry,* and the *New Republic,* among other magazines, as well as in the New Directions anthologies of 1937 and 1938. Revisions were in most cases limited to isolated words and phrases, punctuation, and some changes in title.

The original book opened with the title story, which was followed by *Coriolanus and His Mother.* The third part comprised two groups of poems, "The Repetitive Heart" and "Twenty-four Poems," under the rather diffident general title, "Poems of Experimentation and Imitation." These groups appear in *Summer Knowledge* in reverse order, with the group now first called, incomprehensibly, "The Dreams Which Begin in Responsibilities." This group contains three early poems not in the first collection: "Out of the Watercolored Window, When You Look"; "Someone Is Harshly Coughing as Before," discussed in the last chapter; and "Cambridge, Spring 1937." The fourth part of *In Dreams Begin Responsibilities* contained *Dr. Bergen's*

Belief. The book's dedication is to the poet's first wife, Gertrude Buckman. It is accompanied by the first words of a poem by the Roman emperor Hadrian to his soul, "Animula, vagula, blandula...." A free translation of this poem precedes "Prothalamion."[1]

As Schwartz remarks among his notes to the book, its title derives from an epigraph, "In dreams begins responsibility," which William Butler Yeats placed before his own collection, *Responsibilities* (1914) and attributed to an "old play." A second epigraph, from Confucius, follows: "How am I fallen from myself, for a long time now I have not seen the Prince of Chang in my dreams."[2] It may be that Yeats is referring to his responsibility to realize his dreams in the form of poetry, to keep faith with the innermost life of his soul and with his past, a responsibility that Schwartz recognizes as his own. Also, by echoing Yeats' first epigraph, he links himself to his great and aged contemporary, who was shortly to die.

Many of Schwartz's poems exemplify his strong intellectual bent as he focuses his attention upon the most banal, commonplace details of daily existence and transforms them into a coherent, abstract idea that is inseparable from the observed particulars. For example, where an ordinary insomniac observer might have seen only a play of automobile headlights upon his bedroom ceiling, in a situation of the kind described in "In the Naked Bed, in Plato's Cave," Schwartz finds an analogy to a Platonic parable. If poetry of ideas is to succeed, it must show the harmonious interweaving of observation and abstraction. If the argument of this poem is interesting, it is because one is satisfied by the likeness that the poet sees between a bedroom and the cave of the parable, between a succession of images that at one and the same time faithfully record the facts of an ordinary experience and illustrate a point of view available only through the mediation of the intellect. Schwartz observes of a poem by Allen Tate, "The complication which strengthens the images is often intellectual, that is to say, the bond between the image and the subject depends upon the intellect, which has seen a relationship not given to visual observation, although often framed in visual terms."[3]

Schwartz's attempts to reconcile poetry and abstract thought fail when he uses verse merely as a vehicle for the direct statement of ideas. In *Genesis*, for example, he more often than not betrays the spirit of poetry by using blank verse in iambic pentameter as a convenient, ready-made form for highly intellectualized arguments, some of which, perhaps, he would have been reluctant to state so baldly in prose. The danger to the intellectual poet is in his proneness to see too clearly with his mind. Often liable to the same mistake, Schwartz remarks the "tendency or temptation" on the part of Allen Tate "to grasp the subject too intellectually and thus too abstractly."[4]

Many of Schwarz's early poems reflect ordinary speech and have a subdued, conversational quality. The language tends to be flat and abstract, unemphasized, and casual. The tone is often meditative and detached, reflecting the point of view of an intellectual observer who turns to the common objects and situations of daily life for images and examples with which to embody his thought. In this respect he resembles W. H. Auden, whose influence sometimes shows obtrusively, as does that of Schwartz's two other chief models, Eliot and Yeats.

Schwartz draws close to Eliot in his use of allusions and epigraphs, while in some passages he reflects the subdued, ironic tone of Eliot's musings over human vanity and delusion, as in "Father and Son":

> See the evasions which so many don,
> To flee the guilt of time they become one,
> That is, the one number among masses,
> The one anonymous in the audience,
> The one expressionless in the subway,
> In the subway evening among so many faces. . . .[5]

These lines suggest the Eliot of "Animula," in which the young child is described as

> Rising or falling, grasping at kisses and toys,
> Advancing boldly, sudden to take alarm,
> Retreating to the corner of arm and knee,
> Eager to reassured, taking pleasure
> In the fragrant brilliance of the Christmas tree. . . .[6]

Elsewhere there are echoes of Yeats, as in the lines beginning "For the One Who Would Take Man's Life in His Hands":

> Tiger Christ unsheathed his sword,
> Threw it down, became a lamb.
> Swift spat upon his species, but
> Took two women to his heart.
>
> . . . .
>
> Troy burned for a sea-tax, also for
> Possession of a charming whore.
> What do all examples show?
> What must the finished murderer know?[7]

With their references to Swift and Troy, their sequence of terse, demonstrative instances and abrupt rhythms, and their questioning conclusion, nothing could be closer to Yeats than these lines, unless Yeats himself. Moreover, "Tiger Christ" consciously refers to Eliot's "Gerontion": "In the juvescence of the year/ Came Christ the tiger. . . ."[8]

In prosody the poems tend toward the formal and traditional. Although the iambic pentameter line is the basic unit of many of them, Schwartz sometimes favors lines of trimeter and tetrameter length and in all cases varies the metrical pattern. He uses rhyme, but seldom systematically and often in combination with half-rhyme; and he does not insist upon regular stanzaic divisions. However, the three sonnets of the collection— "The Beautiful American Word, Sure," "The Ghosts of James and Peirce in Harvard Yard," and "O City, City"—follow the traditional pattern almost exactly, and there are other instances of strict formalism.

For the most part, the poems to be considered here were not unduly influenced by the poets in ascendancy at the time; and a number of them have survived the self-imposed stigma of their original subtitle. Seven of them are from the group first entitled "Twenty-four Poems": "The Ballad of the Children of the Czar," "In the Naked Bed, in Plato's Cave," "Father and Son," "Far Rockaway," "Parlez-Vous Français?," "A Young Child and His Pregnant Mother," and "Prothalamion." These are among the most substantial poems of the section; and, like the three city poems and "Socrates' Ghost Must Haunt Me Now," discussed in the last chapter, they illustrate particularly well Schwartz's major themes. The above order is that of *Summer Knowledge* (or *Selected Poems*). The arrangement of the group as a whole was somewhat different in the original collection. Following, there will be a discussion of the eleven poems that make up "The Repetitive Heart."

I Seven Poems

In "The Ballad of the Children of the Czar"[9] Schwartz universalizes the life of the hero of the poem, himself, by showing himself at a moment in his own distant past against the background of the time. He imagines that the children of the last Russian Czar, Nicholas II, are playing with a ball in their father's garden, while he, a two-year-old child back home in Brooklyn, is eating a baked potato in his high chair. It is 1916, the year before the outbreak of the Russian Revolution, in which the children will be assassinated along with the rest of the imperial family. At the end of the poem, the ball rolls beyond their reach. The loss of the ball foreshadows their death: man is not in control of his fate; he is not the arbiter of his happiness or his future. Victims of history, the children must suffer for the guilt of their father. Back home, the hero drops his potato, his "buttered world," which evades his own will.

There is no freedom from the past, and what has been inherited will be passed on. Thus, the poet can say, addressing the Czar in the third section, "I am my father's father,/ You are your children's guilt." This anticipates the close of the fifth section, which refers to all children: "They are their father's fathers,/ The past is inevitable." The earth itself, as described in this same section, "Makes no will glad"; it is "Made for no play, for no children,/ But chasing only itself." In the cyclical repetition of the past, "The innocent are overtaken,/ They are not innocent." The myth of the Trojan War in the third section is another illustration of this fatalistic sentiment: "In history's pity and terror/ The child is Aeneas again.... / Child labor! The child must carry/ His fathers on his back." So Aeneas carried his crippled father Anchises when he fled from Troy.

"In the Naked Bed, in Plato's Cave"[10] is, on the most immediate level of meaning, a record of various impressions—as has been noted—that the narrator receives in his bedroom during a night of broken sleep. There is no overt moral, no statement of general import, until the last lines of the poem, though mention of "Plato's cave" announces at the outset that the poem has a parabolic meaning. According to the Platonic parable from Book 7 of *The Republic,* which underlies Schwartz's poem, the world men know is like a cave in which prisoners have been chained in such a way that they must face a wall upon which they see, cast by the light of a fire, shadows of themselves and of objects passing behind them. These shadows are all they know of reality. Reality itself, the world of essences beyond sense experience, is represented as lying outside the cave, in the sunlight. Men, with their limited knowledge, are like those prisoners.

In the poem, an actual bedroom takes the place of the cave that in Plato is merely a simile, and the world outside is the actual world and not a simile for a reality beyond it. According to this substitution of the literal for the symbolic, Schwartz's meaning seems to be the direct opposite of Plato's: the world in time (and of being in time) *is* reality itself. The narrator of the poem experiences the world in terms of sound and reflected light. Enhanced by reference to the original parable, the terms "reflected," "shaded windows," the surmise that the freights of the trucks passing outside are "covered," and "slanting diagram"—this last phrase especially—take on a metaphorical value. Impressions register with insomniac intensity. Carpenters are hammering (one may wonder why, as it is night); trucks strain uphill. "Troubled," while describing the effect of the wind on the curtains, also refers to the narrator himself. Sometime later, possibly after sleeping and waking again, hearing the abrupt "chop" of the hooves of the milkman's horse and the milkman's laborious "striving up the stair," he leaves his bed, goes to the the window, and looks out.

It is the moment before dawn: night has passed and day has yet to be born. The street is "stony," the buildings stand in their own stillness, the street lamp keeps a "vigil," and the horse waits with "patience." Everything is still. The scene suggests that this pause between night and day is a moment out of time, absolute, like the world of Platonic ideas. "The winter sky's pure capital" drives the narrator back to bed with "exhausted eyes," as if he had looked upon an unbearable absolute reality. The sky is, in fact, the "inexorable blue" of "Socrates' Ghost Must Haunt Me Now." With its purity and stillness this outdoor scene contrasts with the strenuous activity in the first part of the poem, but both answer to the original parable in their different ways.

What might be called the Platonic moment passes, and day begins. The world in time invades the bedroom, insisting upon confrontation: "Shaking wagons, hooves' waterfalls,/ Sounded far off, increasing, louder and nearer./ A car coughed, starting." In this section, the emphasis is upon liquifaction and combustion: "Morning, softly/ Melting the air, lifted the half-covered chair/ From underseas, kindled the looking-glass. ..." This section contrasts to the abrupt, mechanical actions described earlier, for here the flow and fire of time break upon the narrator. At the insistence of a bird that "bubbled and whistled, so!," he returns to full consciousness, "Perplexed, still wet/ With sleep, affectionate, hungry and cold." The song fuses with his own logic. So he must face the reality of existence in time after the "ignorant night." As "the son of man," he must endure the "travail" or birth agony of morning, "the mystery of beginning/ Again and again, while History is unforgiven."

Concern with time is also at the heart of "Father and Son," a dramatic dialogue in which the voice of age and the voice of youth conflict—the father, who sees time as death, and the son, who sees it as "a dancing fire."[11] The father tells his son that the young man is afraid of time and that his fear is guilty fear: "Your guilt is nameless, because its name is time,/ Because its name is death."[12] The son's escapism is futile: "Each moment is dying. You will try to escape/ From melting time and your dissipating soul/ By hiding your head in a warm and dark hole."[13] Redemption from the guilt of time is found only in facing the fact of time, and hence one's death, squarely by means of total self-awareness, by a deliberate commitment to the inescapable self and to the past that lives on as memory:

> You cannot depart and take another name,
> Nor go to sleep with lies. Always the same,
> Always the same self from the ashes of sleep
> Returns with its memories, always, always,
> The phoenix with eight hundred thousand memories![14]

In the last part of the poem the father refers to Hamlet as an "example" to follow: "... only dying/ Did he take up his manhood, the dead's burden,/ Done with evasion, done with sigh-ing,/ Done with revery. Decide that you are dying..../ Act... as if death were now...."[15] The poem closes with his admo-nition: "Be guilty of yourself in the full looking-glass." There is a paradox in this advice which the poem does not exploit—introspection or self-consciousness, as symbolized by the "look-ing-glass," is supposed to lead to action, but more likely than not it becomes a substitute for action, just as it does so often elsewhere in Schwartz's work.

The title of the poem that follows, "Far Rockaway,"[16] is the name of an ocean resort not far from Coney Island, the setting of "In Dreams Begin Responsibilities." Here "The rigor of the weekday is cast aside with shoes,/ With business suits and the traffic's motion...." Returning to the elements, a man can abandon himself to "the passionate sun" or become "drunken in the ocean." However, the real problem of human existence has to do with time, from which there is no escape. The typical bather is indulging in the escapism that the father warns against in the preceding poem. "He is stripped of his class in the bathing-suit,/ He returns to the children digging at summer,/ A melon-like fruit." He loses first his social identity, then his adulthood, and finally his humanity. In the presence of the "eternities of sea and sky," "Time unheard moves and the heart of man is eaten/ Consummately at leisure."

Upon this scene intrudes "the novelist"—that is, the artist, the observer, the introspective man—"tangential on the board-walk," removed from what he sees. Skeptical and questioning, he "seeks his cure of souls in his own anxious gaze"—a reference to the epigraph of the poem, "the cure of souls," attributed to Henry James but in fact a conventional phrase meaning "the spiritual ministry of souls," the duty of a curate or priest. The line is rather obscure, but there is obviously a play on "cure," which in the context of the original phrase means "care." The bathers are concerned with a physical cure, but the observer is interested in the health of the soul. " 'What satisfaction, fruit? What transit, heaven?/ Criminal? justified? arrived at what June?' " What, he may be asking, is the purpose of this existence, this abandonment to time? But the questioning is futile: "That nervous conscience amid the concessions/ Is a haunting, haunted moon." "Conscience" here means consciousness, as in French;

but at the same time, it retains the usual moral denotation.
The word is similarly used in "The World Is a Wedding."

"Parlez-Vous Français?"[17] offers another instance of the conflict between passive existence and the artist's exacerbated
consciousness, or "conscience." "Caesar," speaking on the radio
in a barbershop, promises the men supine in their chairs "Pride,
justice, and the sun/ Brilliant and strong on everyone...."
"Caesar" is probably Hitler, whose hysterical speeches were
sometimes broadcast in America before World War II. In any
case, the poet is concerned with the nature of absolute power.
The voice of "Caesar" triumphs not so much by terrorizing as
by promising bread and circuses, commonplace distractions, and
still with these, "pride" and "justice." He is, in short, appealing
to everything that is slothful and irresponsible in human nature.

Upon this scene enters "the writer merely," who is neglected
in appearance, an outcast with "a three-day beard." Mustering
his courage, he attacks "his enemy," speaking, as Schwartz
acknowledges in a note in the original collection, an English
French, which indicates a bookish rather than a natural contact
with the language that represents in the poem Western civilization. The hero is learned, but he is no more at home in his
acquired culture than he is in America. Flaunting his assumed
foreignness, speaking a language that probably nobody in the
barbershop understands, he deliberately emphasizes his
estrangement.

"Listen!" he cries (to translate): "Most men live lives of quiet
desperation, victims of innumerable intentions. And that man
well knows it." He deals with "dreams and lies." It is he that
wills and chooses, and what he brings is "the end of summer,"
war, and death. This outburst of "the foreigner" is greeted with
mocking incomprehension. However, even if he had spoken in
English, he would have seemed essentially foreign since the
crowd would not have understood his message, which begins,
moreover, with an awkward French translation of a well-known
observation by that more serene native American foreigner,
Thoreau.[18]

"A Young Child and His Pregnant Mother"[19] describes the
crisis that comes to every individual when he is forced to recog-
nize himself as such—when he becomes aware that he is unique
and alone in the world and that other individuals exist besides

himself. Approaching this critical moment of early childhood, the subject of the poem vaguely apprehends that he is about to lose his primacy in his mother's affections and that he is no longer a part of her. Though the poem is essentially psychological, it also has a metaphysical dimension. The hero's initial estrangement, "his exile from his mother," is "measured by his distance from the sky," the infinitely remote sky which throughout Schwartz's work appears as a symbol of the absolute.

Unlike the sky, which has a masculine aspect (as the abode of God and as associated with the hero's own "towering" father in the eighth couplet), "Nature is mountainous,/ Mysterious, and submarine." It is maternal and embracing, womblike. Mention of the subway, which follows immediately, hints at the exile and estrangement that await him: "Between the grate,/ Dropping his penny, he learned out all loss,/ The irretrievable cent of fate. . . ."

Now, confronting "this newest of the mysteries," his mother's pregnancy, he senses that the days of his childhood are numbered. His mother is "much too fat and absentminded,/ Gazing far past his face, careless of him. . . ." No longer will he find his existence and his identity confirmed in her eyes. ". . . soon the night will be too dark, the spring/ Too late, desire strange, and time too fast,/ This first estrangement is a gradual thing. . . ." Desire will no longer be one with immediate satisfaction, and time will be contrary to the self. The "first estrangement" foreshadows the absolute estrangement described at the end of the poem. The following couplet renders the child's bewilderment at his mother's change: "(His mother once so svelte, so often sick;/ Towering father did this: what a trick!)" The last phrase suggests both magic and deception on the part of the father.

Leaving the child's point of view and returning to general statement, the poet observes that the hero's incipient rivalry with his unborn brother is an instance of human enmity: "All men are enemies: thus even brothers/ Can separate each other from their mothers!" This separation describes the abiding condition of man, his aloneness in the world, which can be stated in the very terms of self-awareness that end the poem, can be "spoken in two vowels, I am I."

With the title "Prothalamion," this poem recalls Spenser's poem written for the marriage of the daughters of the Earl of

Worcester. In subject, Schwartz's work also recalls Spenser's
"Epithalamion"; for Schwartz is writing about his own forth-
coming marriage. The opening strophes of the poem approach
the theme of marriage with ceremonial gravity and reverence.
It is a "feast of bondage and unity," a "great piety." It is, therefore, time to be honest, to put aside "masks" and "enigmatic
clothes." The poet reveals his weakness, his need to be loved
and remembered, when he recalls the gift of an apple to a little
girl, declaring that "my name/ Is fed like a raving fire, insati-
ate still." He thus confesses his egoism, but he assures his bride
that her beauty will make him forget himself.

He will forget "the speech my mother made/ In a restaurant, trapping my father there/ At dinner with his whore." This
scene is described in detail in *Genesis*, and there can be little
doubt that it is autobiographical. The memory of his mother's
"spoken rage" entered into his life, and he admits that her
"rhetoric/ Has charmed my various tongue." This rhetoric of
accusation he must forget above all, for "Love's metric seeks a
rhyme more pure and sure." Death, too, which the poet first
confronted "at thirteen when a little girl died," must be forgotten in the celebration of love, even if daylight brings, as it
must, the sense of "nothingness."

There follows now, as a kind of charm against loneliness and
this sense of nothingness, several strophes of invocation that are
at once playful and somber. The poet invites Freud and Marx
to the wedding feast to "mark out the masks that face us there."
For, of all evils, none is worse than self-deception. He invokes
Mozart, who represents "the irreducible incorruptible good/
Risen past birth and death, though he is dead,"[20] and he sum-
mons members of the world at large. Each must bring some
emblem or perform some act that will help to define the nature
of the marriage: its delight, its purity, its frailty.

The invited include jewelers, children eating ice cream,
acrobats, the stars, mathematicians, florists, and "the charming
bird for ignorant song," no doubt the nightingale. The catalog
reaches its climax with an address to the goddess Athena, perhaps as the patroness of intellectuals. Modernized, with her
"tired beauty"—from thinking too much?—she is to appear in
a bathing suit, and the poet will fraternally carry her symbol,
a white owl. Finally, the poet calls upon Robinson Crusoe, "to

utter the emotion/ Of finding Friday, no longer alone," and Charlie Chaplin, "muse of the curbstone,/ Mummer of hope."

But the names of Crusoe and Chaplin, even as the poet invokes them, bring in again the awareness of loneliness; and in the next strophe he returns to the initial situation of the poem. Awakening from his dream, he exclaims, "But this is fantastic and pitiful,/ And no one comes, none will, we are alone. . . ." In the remainder of the poem, he tries to come to grips with this all but overwhelming problem of loneliness. He pledges to care for his bride with body and soul, but he reminds her that the body is "heavy"—is, in fact, "the heavy bear" of the poem by that name. To marry is to add to the burden of one's own mortality that of the beloved and to take upon oneself "time like a fate/ Near as my heart, dark when I marry you."[21]

The lines that follow suggest that the poet loses touch with solid reality in the crisis of his choice. "Love is inexhaustible and full of fear." He seeks the reassurance of the everyday world, "The look of actuality, the certainty/ Of those who run down stairs and drive a car." To relieve their loneliness, the lovers must ceremoniously become a world in themselves: ". . . let us/ Affirm the other's self, and be/ The other's audience, the other's state,/ Each to the other his sonorous fame."

The poet, afraid of his variable personality, anticipates the fear of his bride when she will discover that he can be either "lion or lamb" and become aware of the dark, irrational side to his nature—"the daemon breathing heavily/ His sense of ignorance, his wish to die,/ For I am nothing because my circus self/ Divides its love a million times." In the last strophe he calls himself "the octopus in love with God"—an image that carries on the idea of formlessness and division. As the octopus issues ink, so does his mind issue "its own darkness." The final invocation of the poem is to this "God of my perfect ignorance" for help in his marriage—to a God conceived in the darkness of his doubt rather than in the clarity of certain faith.[22]

II *The Repetitive Heart: Poems in Imitation of the Fugue*

This group of poems came first in *In Dreams Begin Responsibilities*, but they retain their original order in *Summer Knowledge* (or *Selected Poems*), and only the slightest changes have been made in the text, variations in spelling. Originally, the poems were numbered rather than titled with first lines, except for the last, which was called "Dedication in Time," which is more appropriate than the present "Time's Dedication." The subtitle of the group in the first collection was slightly different: "Eleven Poems in Imitation of the Fugue Form."

The poems are interesting, first of all, because of their form, a poetic equivalent of the musical fugue. Schwartz notes in *In Dreams Begin Responsibilities* that they might more accurately be called poems in a form suggested by the fugue since it is impossible to reproduce counterpoint in language. It is impossible because words must occur one by one in time, while in the fugue interwoven melodies, taken up by one voice after another, develop simultaneously. Schwartz achieves the effect of simultaneity by interweaving different strands of verse. One may be interrupted by another, then completed later, and interrupt in its turn the sequence of the second verse, which in turn is completed. "Calmly We Walk through This April's Day" offers a simple example:

> The children shouting are bright as they run
> (This is the school in which they learn...)
> Ravished entirely in their passing play!
> (...that time is the fire in which they burn.)

In these poems Schwartz makes good use of alliteration and various forms of rhyme. Noteworthy is the consonance of "wind" and "mind" in "Will You Perhaps Consent To Be," and the relationship between "choices," "chosen faces," and "circumstances" in "All Clowns Are Masked and All *Personae*," a play of sound equivalent to musical variation. All of these poems suggest reiteration and development by string instruments, and there is an effect as of stroking bows.

This elaborate imitation is more than surface virtuosity. Schwartz's re-creation of the fugue is justified as a formal exposition of the theme of these poems, which the title of the group announces. "Heart" signifies mortality, and "repetitive" refers not only to the beat of the actual heart but also to existence in time. These associations are explicit in "Prothalamion," where the poet speaks of "time like a fate/ Near as my heart." Repetition is akin to circularity and cyclical movement. In the first poem of the series, "All of Us Always Turning Away for Solace," the heart is "The bouncing ball you turned from for solace."

Time, the central presence of these poems, is given a formal order, as in music. The poems create the effect of describing complete circles. Furthermore, the suggestion of musical counterpoint is in keeping with the dialectical progression of these poems, in which different sets of values, ideas, and the like, playing together, reach an ultimate harmony.

The first poem of the series, "All of Us Always Turning Away for Solace,"[23] recalls both "Father and Son" and "Far Rockaway"; for it describes the futile attempt to escape from self-awareness by means of distractions. The image of the ball recalls "The Ballad of the Children of the Czar." Capricious and at the same time mechanical, the ball stands for both the object of human desire and, as the last line ironically shows, the heart itself— the dreaded mortality that man must carry with him even as he tries to escape it.

In "Will You Perhaps Consent To Be,"[24] a love poem, the wind symbolizes the restlessness of the will that "Lusts for Paris, Crete and Pergamus,/ Is suddenly off for Paris and Chicago,/ Judaea, San Francisco, the Midi...." Here again flight from the self is the subject, flight balanced by return to the loved girl, "My many-branched, small and dearest tree." The image suggests both tenderness and strength, for the tree is at once small and yielding and deeply rooted in one spot. However, the tree is also "the very rack and crucifix of winter" upon which the winter's "ice-caressing wind" will immolate itself.

"All Clowns Are Masked and All *Personae*"[25] considers the possibility of choice and its relation to what is determined. The first strophe of the poem states the existence of choice only to deny it dialectically: Men are clowns in the comedy played upon the stage of life. All *personae*, all the characters of this comedy, apparently "flow from choices" and appear to have "chosen faces." However, these are "circumstances," and so resemble things that are not of their choosing; they are "Given, like a tendency/ To colds or like blond hair and wealth,/ Or war and peace or gifts for mathematics...." They "stick to us/ In time," and even Socrates, according to the famous syllogism, is "mortal." The following strophe elaborates these opposing points of view. "... we have gifts which interrupt our choices,/

And all our choices grasp in Blind Man's Buff...." No one can see the results of what he apparently does choose. However, he must live while he can: "But save your soul! Only the past is immortal."

The final strophe tries to reconcile choice and circumstances. Travel and other escapes may bring happiness, but "he who chooses chooses what is given,/ He who chooses is ignorant of Choice...." Acting with the vital illusion of choice in the midst of blindness, one should choose the most fruitful and promising thing, love, out of which the future will grow inexhaustibly.

"Calmly We Walk through This April's Day"[26] considers the identity of the self that persists through or changes in time and the possibility that memory may "restore again and again/ The smallest color of the smallest day...." As the poet walks down a street with a friend, he is conscious of "Metropolitan poetry here and there," noticing the "pauper and *rentier*" together. The scene is active, explosive even, with "the screaming children, the motor-car/ Fugitive about us, running away...." Everything is propelled by time. Thought of number makes him consider the date, thought of the date leads him to consider mortality. What will survive "besides the photo and the memory?"

The next strophe takes up the problem of identity: "What is the self amid this blaze?/ What am I now that I was then/ Which I shall suffer and act again...." The final strophe considers the dead: do they still, and where do they still exist, those who have no place in the present, yet who live on in memory? The refrain lines, together for the first time, round out the poem: "Time is the school in which we learn,/ Time is the fire in which we burn."

"Dogs Are Shakespearean, Children Are Strangers,"[27] evokes the fundamental strangeness of existence, which defies analysis. Though Freud, Wordsworth (of the "Intimations of Immortality"), angels, and Platonists try to define the natures of children and dogs—here symbolic of elemental life—they must all fail; for their points of view are too narrow and conflict with one another. Men are all "strangers," and so men are "Shakespearean." This may mean that their lives fit no theory, and that only Shakespeare can do justice to the ultimate mystery of existence, which "we live behind our unseen faces,/ ... howling or dancing out our souls/ In beating syllables before the curtain...."

The meaning of the poem that follows, "Do the Others Speak of Me Mockingly, Maliciously?"[28] is self-evident: the poet deplores backbiting and duplicity, and he tells of his need for love. If the poem has any interest, it is because it expresses the paranoid fears that were already afflicting Schwartz at an early age: "Do they whisper behind my back? Do they speak/ Of my clumsiness? Do they laugh at me,/ Mimicking my gestures, retailing my shame?/ I'll whirl about, denounce them, saying/ That they are shameless, they are treacherous...."

"I Am to My Own Heart Merely a Serf"[29] describes the ritual boredom of daily life in the city, and again the heart represents mortality in all of its darkness and heaviness. The poet is "sick of its cruel rule, as sick/ As one is sick of chewing gum all day...." At times, sleep brings release and comfort; at other times, he takes his obsessions into his dreams, where he must perform "chores impossible and heavy," including the familiar chore of carrying the past—"The carriage of my father on my back,/ Last summer, 1910, and my own people"—and endless acts of counting and identification, the repetitive, obsessive acts of one who is bound to his own heart in time.

"Abraham and Orpheus, Be With Me Now,"[30] invokes the patriarch who was stayed from sacrificing his son by an angel of the Lord, and Orpheus, who lost Eurydice to death with a backward glance—two that loved, who knew the closeness of their love to death, "How poised on nothing, weighted on the air,/ The touched, seen substance, the substance of care...." The second strophe of the poem brings in the great antagonist, time. Love is close to death; and time that "goes round and round" and that "circles in its idiot defeat" is the enemy of everything. Existence, ruled by time, pursues an endless, exhausting circle.

In the final strophe, the poet realizes that it is impossible to remain aloof from life: "Love sucked me to the moving street below...." He is caught in the whirl of time. He sees "the price of care," though he knows that "time which circles dissipates all care...." Love is a great responsibility, and brings its own darkness, for "every solid thing must shadow in the light...." In closing the poem, the poet again invokes the patriarch and the hero who knew the terror of love and whose "learned presence" may therefore protect him in his own time of need.

"The Heavy Bear Who Goes With Me"[31] is a long metaphor in which, as already observed, the bear represents the body and, by extension, the heaviness of existence in time. The bear is a performing one, and a suggestion of the circus pervades the poem. This "hungry beating brutish one," full of desire and appetite, has only one fear, death. He "Trembles to think that his quivering meat/ Must finally wince to nothing at all." The bear "perplexes and affronts with his own darkness,/ The secret life of belly and bone,/ Opaque, too near, my private, yet unknown...."

In contrast to this heaviness and opacity, there is a suspected spiritual reality that the poet cannot experience because the bear is "a stupid clown of the spirit's motive." He longs for a purer way of living, for communion with the woman he loves; but the bear is always in the way. He "stretches to embrace the very dear/ With whom I would walk without him near...." He drags the poet "with him in his mouthing care,/ Amid the hundred million of his kind,/ The scrimmage of appetite everywhere." This last line, which ends the poem, suggests that life is a game like football, and thus recalls the first poem of the series. The epigraph, "the withness of the body," is attributed in *In Dreams Begin Responsibilities* to Alfred North Whitehead.

"A Dog Named Ego, the Snowflakes as Kisses"[32] resembles "The Heavy Bear" in theme; for the poet again deals with the duality of the body and the spirit. As its name shows, the dog Ego is the self; and the image suggests that the self is inseparable from instinctive desire. The dog is not, like the bear, an intruder, apart from the self. At the same time, when one considers the dog-master relationship, and the other ego of the poem, "I," or the narrator, one realizes that the self here has two aspects. The master of the dog provides another image of the self—as the observer of its own actions, the ego in the act of self-awareness. The poem thus dramatizes the subject-object relationship that is fundamental in Schwartz's work.

While out for a walk on a December evening, both master and dog are excited by the spectacle of falling snow. Ego, "the stranger, unknown,/ With me, near me," pursues the snowflakes; the master passively feels them falling upon his face "as kisses." "One kissed me, two kissed me! So many died!/ While Ego barked at them, swallowed their touch. . . ." The self here has one goal—to experience the scattered bits, the intimations of a transcendent reality, that are "falling from some place half believed and unknown." Ironically, the hungering self destroys that which it seeks, and which it senses, moreover, erotically. The poem thus states the relationship between the physical and the spiritual more subtly than "The Heavy Bear," which conventionally describes the separation and the opposition of the two.

The outcome of the poem is that Ego is led far from his master in pursuit of the snowflakes. The self, this may mean, lured away by the evasive illusion of the snowfall, has lost itself. The narrator, desolate, becomes aware that night has "collapsed" about him. The reiterated ending, "And left me no recourse, far from my home," suggests both self-alienation and alienation from the object of the quest.

Like "The Heavy Bear," "A Dog Named Ego" has been much anthologized, and deservedly so. The poem is the most complex of the series, a work of substance presented with a technical virtuosity that reconciles opposing forces on several levels to simulate a musical harmony. The opposites of instinctive desire and yearning for a transcendent reality, the self seen in two aspects, the voice of Ego intertwining with a musical description of the falling snow—all are balanced and brought together within the framework of a strong poetic structure.

"Time's Dedication,"[33] though not the equal of "A Dog Named Ego," appropriately ends the series. Again, the theme is time itself. One must learn to accept time, to move with it: "We cannot stand still: time is dying,/ We are dying: Time is farewell!" For two lovers, release from the tyranny of time may be to move through it together at the same pace:

> Then we will be well, parallel and equal,
> Running together down the macadam road,
> Walking together,
> Controlling our pace before we get old. . . .

The final image—of Charlie Chaplin walking with his "orphan sister"—recalls the ending of an old-time movie. Schwartz was fond of references to motion pictures. The silent screen provided him with the central metaphor of his title story, "In Dreams Begin Responsibilities," which is discussed in the next chapter with other works that have or suggest a theatrical setting.

CHAPTER 5

"In the Darkened Theater's Plays"

THE first three of the five pieces to be considered in this chapter appeared in *In Dreams Begin Responsibilities*: the title story of the collection; *Coriolanus and His Mother*; and *Dr. Bergen's Belief*, which has never been reprinted. *Shenandoah* and *Genesis* complete the list. The arrangement of the discussion is chronological, but these works belong together for a more cogent reason. All of them establish a relationship between a scene of action and a spectator, or spectators, concerned with that action—between event on the one hand and witness on the other.

Dr. Bergen's Belief and *Shenandoah* are, in fact, plays, and the other works are theatrical in spirit. The two plays, moreover, not only assume an audience, but also set up a play-audience relationship onstage. In the first play, a group of characters gathered in a living room watch the actions of another group assembled on a terrace beyond; in *Shenandoah* the hero is present onstage as a commentator on the play, in which he is present as a baby. The narrator of "In Dreams Begin Responsibilities" dreams that he is in a movie house watching a film about the engagement of his parents. A dream theater is also the setting for a performance of Shakespeare in *Coriolanus and His Mother*, which is watched by the narrator and the ghosts of several great men; and *Genesis* has its own ghostly observers and its scene of action, the life story of its hero. *Genesis* also abounds in metaphors that compare the hero's life and creation itself to a drama. Schwartz thus gives a form to the polarities of experience and consciousness, or knowledge, and to the conflicts and ironies brought about by their encounter.

With the exception of the story, all of these works contain both prose and verse. In *Shenandoah* and in *Genesis*, prose is used for the main action; verse, for the commentary. In *Dr. Bergen's Belief*, verse appears mainly in the prologue. *Coriolanus and His Mother* is in blank verse that often incorporates or paraphrases Shakespeare's own lines, while the speeches between the acts are in prose. This alternation from the one form to the other represents, in most cases, a shift in levels of dramatic reality.

The use of both prose and verse, with a tendency of the first to take on the cadences of free verse, indicates that Schwartz does not regard the differences between the two forms as essential. For him, the generic term for the writer is "poet." Whatever the form, prose or verse, poetry is all in the vision. In no work of Schwartz's is it more evident than in the title story of his first collection, a narrative that nevertheless unfolds quietly and prosaically, without lyrical emphasis—in such a way, in fact, as to set off an underlying emotional intensity.

I *"In Dreams Begin Responsibilities"*

Although it is one of his earliest stories, Schwartz never surpassed "In Dreams Begin Responsibilities" (1938). The quietness of the narration heightens the hero's growing involvement in his dream, a tormenting dream about a crucial event, the engagement of his parents, which takes the form of an old movie whose characters have undergone a comic stylization that is at the same time pathetic. The narrator grieves for them and for himself also as he sees in retrospect the event that decided his own being. Projecting himself into the film, his dream within a dream, he makes inferences and states facts that a silent movie could not give. At two points, he tries to affect the action: once, to break the engagement, for he does not want to be born; and again to resolve an argument between his father and mother, the initial and portentous quarrel of their life together. He becomes more and more aware that he is a member of an audience. Finally, he is escorted from the theater by an usher whose voice becomes that of his own growing consciousness. The time of the story is that of dream: on the one hand, is the unreal past; on the other, the unreal present.

No other story of Schwartz's so well embodies his sense of the pastness of the past, its comic superannuation. The film seems to be "an old Biograph one, in which the actors are dressed in ridiculously old-fashioned clothes, and one flash succeeds another with sudden jumps. The actors too seem to jump about and walk too fast. The shots themselves are full of dots and rays, as if it were raining when the picture was photographed. The light is bad."[1] That it might actually have been raining when the film was made emphasizes the unreality of the scene.

The mood of this opening description is sustained throughout the story, and not only by images of the obsolete, such as the automobile in the first part that looks like "an enormous upholstered sofa,"[2] but also by the use of simple declarative sentences that follow one another with mechanical regularity. Almost all of the paragraphs of the first part begin with "my father," who is on his way to the house of the narrator's mother. Furthermore, the movements and thought processes of the dream figures reflect the abrupt, quick pace of a silent movie.

The narrator sometimes infers what goes on in the minds of his characters, as when he says, "It is evident that the respect in which my father is held in this household is tempered by a good deal of mirth."[3] Throughout the story, there is a suggestion of pantomimic expressiveness that would favor such inferences. The narrator also reports thoughts and unheard conversations. In the first part, for example, he says that his father, nervous about proposing marriage, "reassures himself by thinking of the big men he admires who are married: William Randolph Hearst, and William Howard Taft, who has just become President of the United States."[4] Besides revealing his father's character, this passage relates the private, family history to the history of the time.

The dreamer is active from the first, providing the exact date, "Sunday afternoon, June 12th, 1909," which he fixes after the initial moment of doubt that begins the story, "I think it is the year 1909."[5] He thus passes into his dream, assuming the dreamer's omniscience. He also provides sensory details that would not be in a silent, black-and-white film. In the first part, "the street-car's noises emphasize the quiet of the holiday." The doorbell is "loud."[6] Elsewhere there are details of color.

Part two describes his father's reception at the house of his mother's family, and the couple's departure for Coney Island, where they are to have dinner. This section is brief, containing only four paragraphs, but it is poetically rich and complex. The film breaks off at a crucial point: the narrator's grandfather "is worried; he is afraid that my father will not make a good husband for his oldest daughter."[7] With this break, the narrator returns to self-awareness, and an awareness of the audience, which claps impatiently. Throughout the story, each of his involvements has as its reaction a return to himself.

When the movie starts up again, the part just shown is repeated: time is played over, as if to emphasize the grandfather's foreboding, which the narrator knows is justified. The section ends with the breakdown of the narrator himself: he bursts into tears over a stupid and yet pathetic conversation between his father and mother, who have boarded a "street-car" en route to Coney Island. A "determined old lady" sitting next to him reproves him with a look, and he stops weeping, self-indulgently licking a tear from his lips. When he returns to the movie, he sees his parents getting off at "the last stop, Coney Island."[8]

In this second part, a powerful sentence conveys the dreamer's sense of time. He wonders why his older uncle is not present in the family group, and realizes that it is because he will shortly be dead. "He is studying in his bedroom upstairs, studying for his final examination at the College of the City of New York, having been dead of rapid pneumonia for the last twenty-one years."[9] The causality of dream, with the shift of tenses, produces an effect of great poignancy; while "final" and "rapid" have ominous connotations. This single sentence contains the essence of Schwartz's tragic awareness of time.

In the third part, the pair are seen on the boardwalk of the Coney Island of yesteryear, idly talking and surveying the scene. The narrator's father goes off to buy peanuts, and his mother "remains at the rail and stares at the ocean. The ocean seems merry to her; it pointedly sparkles and again and again the pony waves are released." The crowd shares her complacency. "The tide does not reach as far as the boardwalk, and the strollers would feel no danger if it did." When his father returns, the two of them "absently stare at the ocean," unaware of its elemental and destructive power.

For the narrator, however, the scene is terrifying. The ocean grows rough as he watches, reflecting his subjective involvement; and he is overwhelmed by the menacing beauty of the waves. But his parents remain indifferent, and they are also unaware of the force of the sun, whose "lightning" strikes overhead. "But I stare at the terrible sun which breaks up sight, and the fatal, merciless, passionate ocean, I forget my parents." Shocked by their indifference to the universal forces of life, he begins to weep once more. The old lady now tries to console him, telling him that it is "only a movie." He is taking his dream of the past too seriously. The past may be wept over, but it is a fiction after all.[10]

The fourth part describes the father's proposal, and gives the mother's words of excited acceptance, "It's all I've wanted from the moment I saw you," the first direct speech of any length in what is supposed to be a silent movie; as such, the speech probably reflects the depths of the narrator's emotional involvement in the action. Since these fateful words will determine his life, his first attempt to alter the course of the action follows. Totally immersed in the past, he speaks out in turn, warning his parents not to marry: "Don't do it. It's not too late to change your minds, both of you. Nothing good will come of it, only remorse, hatred, scandal, and two children whose characters are monstrous."

What is terrible beyond the narrator's confusion of the past and the present is his wish not to be born, his protest against his own life. His outcry angers the audience, which perhaps represents society, possibly enraged more by his nihilism than by the disturbance itself. An usher hurries toward him; and the old lady, a mother figure, warns him with comic severity: "'Be quiet. You'll be put out, and you paid thirty-five cents to come in.'" The past may be "only a movie," and not a very expensive one at that, even at the time; but, after all, he has chosen to watch it, it is his own dream.[11] This part of the story is full of images and sensations of mechanical motion, such as the merry-go-round that his parents ride to the music of a hand organ. In a restaurant afterward, the father is swept toward his proposal by the frenzy of music and dancers; and he surrenders mindlessly to the demands of the future.

When the narrator's outrage subsides, he returns to the film "with thirsty interest, like a child who wants to maintain his sulk although offered the bribe of candy."[12] The action of the fifth part takes place in a photographer's booth where his father and mother are having their picture taken, a photograph within the series of photographs that is the film itself. Again there is foreboding about the future of the marriage, which the photographer himself feels: "He feels with certainty that somehow there is something wrong in their pose." But when he tries to arrange the couple better, because of his interest in making "beautiful pictures," the father becomes impatient; and the picture is finally taken in haste "with my father's smile turned to a grimace and my mother's bright and false." The camera has caught them in a graceless, constrained pose that is a portent of their future together. The photographer, with whom the narrator has identified, feeling for a moment "quite hopeful," as if the past could after all be changed for the better, represents the artist in his desire for beauty and order, which the father willfully frustrates. The esthetic failure of the photograph betokens the moral failure of the marriage to come.[13]

The setting of the sixth part, the last, is a fortune-teller's booth "which is in a way like the photographer's, since it is draped in black cloth [like the photographer's camera] and its light is shadowed." The light in the photographer's booth is mauve. Both mauve and black represent mourning. What is to be mourned is the future itself, symbolized by the fortune-teller, "a fat, short woman" in bogus "Oriental robes," who is as ludicrous and outlandish as everyone else in the story but is also sinister. The parents quarrel outside the booth, for the father does not want to know the future: he would really like to abandon his fiancée at the very beginning of their engagement. He finally consents to go in, but he stalks out angrily after the reading has begun. The parents' quarrel is, in fact, the prediction. When the mother wants to join the father, the fortune-teller holds her back, as if with a motive opposite to that of the photographer, to guarantee the unhappy future of discord.

Shocked, the narrator again shouts at his father and mother, trying to "communicate" his "terrible fear." Reconciled now to the inevitability of their marriage, he wants to heal this first, portentous rift. The audience turns to stare at him, the old lady pleads with him, and the usher of the theater lectures him and ejects him from his dream of the past into the present, the moment of manhood, "the bleak winter morning of my 21st birthday, the windowsill shining with its lip of snow, and the morning already begun."[14] Awakening from the womblike theater of dream, he must face the challenges and responsibilities of the future. The morning is "bleak" and yet, in its snowy purity, promising.

II Coriolanus and His Mother

The Roman general Caius Marcius (or Martius) Coriolanus (fl. late fifth century B.C.), Plutarch's and Shakespeare's hero, appealed to Schwartz as the very embodiment of individuality. Isolated from the crowd by his lonely pride, he is faithful only to his own ideals. His name, derived from the Volscian town Corioli, which he conquered, reflects his uniqueness. In Schwartz's lines in *Coriolanus and His Mother* (1938), the name is a "new word, new syllable, new tone for his/ Intense selfhood to breathe and whisper...."[15] Moreover, forced to choose between Rome, personified by his mother, Volumnia, and allegiance to the Volscian general Aufidius, to whom he turns after banishment from the city because of his excessive pride, Coriolanus represents the self confronting a choice between the claims of the past and an independent future.

The setting of Shakespeare's play, in Schwartz's interpretation, is human nature itself, seen in an historical light:

> The curtain
> Rises on the heart of man,
> Rome, Rome,
> The history-ridden arena....[16]

The play on the stage of the dream theater is watched by a boy, the poet's alter ego, and five ghosts. Between the acts the hero is onstage as a speaker of parables. Four of the ghosts are Marx, Freud,[17] Aristotle, and Beethoven, whose "Coriolanus Overture" is played during the performance. The fifth ghost is "small" and "anonymous," and his presence arouses "an unknown fear" in the hero.[18] Toward the end of the play, he asks, " 'Who is the white masked one who said no word?' " Aristotle answers:

"He is the one who saw what you did not!
He is the one who heard what you did not,"
. . . .
"He is the one you do not know, my dear."[19]

This fifth ghost has a view of reality that the others do not share.
His presence seems to show that all interpretation, even that of
the learned and wise, is relative and partial, that reality eludes
analysis. By his inscrutable witness, the fifth ghost suggests
the limitations of knowledge. Knowledge is limited in another
way, for the great spectators of the play are "ghosts being
possessed by consciousness,/ Consumed by memory, and powerless."[20] For them, as for the rest of Schwartz's obsessively conscious observers, the price of knowledge is impotence to act.

Beethoven broods throughout the performance, his mood
transmitted by his music; and Marx, Freud, and Aristotle comment frequently upon the action. Aristotle's commentary follows his definition of tragedy in his *Poetics,* as, for example,
when Coriolanus decides to ally himself with the Volscians:
" 'This is the turning-point,' said Aristotle,/ 'This the peripety,
he now has done/ All that a man can do, committed his will/
Once and for all, purchased his only fate.' "[21] Marx, of course,
gives an economic interpretation to events, as when he comments upon the willingness of the poor of Rome to forget their
claims and take up arms against the hostile Voscians: " 'In war's
magnified ache, brilliantly blared,/ The poor mistake their
grandeur and their grief;/ Adding their weakness, they affirm
the state,/ The stranger's grain, the stranger's wealth is seized!' "[22]

Above all, for Schwartz, Shakespeare's *Coriolanus* invites a
Freudian interpretation. In spite of his heroic strength Coriolanus is bound to his mother, and because of her he finally
breaks his fealty to his enemy-friend, Aufidius. Aufidius' epithets
of outrage, "thou boy of tears," "Boy! O slave!"[23] sting the hero
into an awareness of his degradation. Early in the performance
Freud comments on Volumnia's pride in her son's military
prowess: " 'This is the origin, this, this is the place,/ Mother in
love with son and son with her,/ And this aloneness in the womb
began. . . .' " Marx rejoins, " 'Not that poor widow, but society/
Nursed him to being, taught him what to be. . . .' "[24]

In any case, Schwartz's Coriolanus is narcissistic. He has a

"Narcissus baritone." After his victory over the Volscians at Corioli, he regards those who cheer him as the mirror of his glory: "Fame [is] the huge face confronting every man/ Who walks amid his fellows, finding in them/ The audience of his play and satisfaction." This desire for fame is Coriolanus' "secret vice." Applauded, he is "enormously gratified and therefore shamed." He thinks that the crowd is unworthy to praise him: "No one may touch him, none; no one reward him,/ Pay him. His self must be self-fed. He is/ His own, not theirs."[25] His apparent modesty is actually the effect of excessive pride.

In the next to the last prose interlude, "Choose," which describes his wanderings after leaving Rome, Coriolanus is called "Narcissus, Brutus, Judas"—he is a traitor and self-lover. Absolutely alone now, having "attained to the emptiness for which he had striven," he stares at his face in a pool of water, self-regarding. At this moment "of vision and decision," of self-scrutiny, "his mother's face replaces his own" in the water; and she tells him " 'You cannot depart from me. You are nothing apart from me, you do not exist without me.... I am your mother or Rome.' " Still, she insists, he has freedom of choice: " '... your individuality grasps the uniqueness of each moment. This surpasses me. This is your freedom. Choose!' "[26] The hero is bound to the past, the claims of blood and society, yet at the same time he is free insofar as he is a distinct individual. The last prose interlude, "He Is a Person," summarizes this argument.

These prose passages of *Coriolanus and His Mother* add to the commentary that the ghosts themselves provide. Earlier ones, "Pleasure," "Justice," and "There Was a City," are parables tangential to the main theme of the drama. The influence of Kafka is noticeable here, as it is in "The Statues." The interludes as a group are likely to be more interesting to the reader than the verse, which follows a rigid iambic pattern and presents abstract speeches that Louise Bogan called "more pompous than illuminating."[27]

More objectionable is Schwartz's "garbled Shakespeare."[28] He paraphrases passages from *Coriolanus* arbitrarily, sometimes putting lines in the mouths of characters different from those who speak them in the play. In Act 4, Scene 4, of Shakespeare, for example, the Roman soldiers announce to their general, Lartius, that Coriolanus is "slain, sir, doubtless."[29] Schwartz,

who has a messenger with a megaphone report this speech (paraphrase is interspersed with anachronisms and modern diction
as well), assigns it to Lartius himself, and with a difference.
" ' "Slain!/ Slain doubtless," says our general. . . .' "[30] Farther on
Lartius—and not the general Cominius, as in the play—permits
Coriolanus to attack the Volscians once more. And again, Lartius, and not Cominius, in Schwartz's paraphrase, gives the hero
"ten times his proper share of all/ Won on the field. . . ."[31]
Shakespeare writes: ". . . of all/ The treasure, in this field
achiev'd and city,/ We render you the tenth. . . ."[32] Schwartz
purposelessly distorts the original.

Much of *Coriolanus and His Mother* is incomprehensible without continual reference to the play; but such a comparison only
shows that Schwartz often diverges from the original without
justification, and that many passages are arbitrary paraphrases.
What is in question is not the poet's privilege to play upon an
original text and to introduce contemporary language and allusions, but rather the careless arrogance with which he does so
in this instance.

III   Dr. Bergen's Belief

In the brief play, *Dr. Bergen's Belief* (1938), the "belief,"
though founded upon intuition, is austerely intellectual in ritual
and practice. According to the doctor, God, the supreme intelligence, is to be approached and emulated by means of a fas-
tidious effort to possess experience and to overcome time with
maximum consciousness. With his patriarchal severity, the doctor resembles the father in the dialogue poem, "Father and Son."

The play is set in Dr. Bergen's terrace apartment. It is
preceded by a prologue in verse, spoken by the doctor himself
before a mirror in an empty room. He laments the absurdity of
a universe without God, here called Santa Claus. The doctor has
an existentialist view of the world: "One knows that heaven
is epiphenomenal,/ Rising from peaked musicians with bad
complexions." Nevertheless, he declares that he does know God
in part, "the dream behind the dream," "the Santa Claus of the
obsessed, obscene heart."[33]

The play itself opens with another monologue, by Anthony,
the lover of Eleanor Bergen, a daughter of the doctor, who three

months before had killed herself for unknown reasons. Baffled and despondent, Anthony accuses her father and his disciples of being "self-regarding, self-gratifying, self-conscious," and of using the girl's suicide for their own purposes; for they believe that she died to be a "witness" to the truth of her father's doctrine of immortality.[34] After Anthony's exit, a dialogue ensues between the doctor's wife and a psychiatrist, Dr. Newman, whom she has called upon for help; for she fears that her husband may be insane and that he is being used by some of his disciples. Dr. Newman assures her that Dr. Bergen is not really mad; he is only confused and unhappy because of "the kind of world in which we now exist," where everything is "becoming strange, repugnant, too difficult...."[35] He reveals that Eleanor had come to him for help. He is at the point of telling more, when Dr. Bergen enters with his disciples and invites him to stay to watch the ceremony about to begin.

The group goes to the terrace and sits down around a long table. A ritualistic dialogue follows between the doctor and the others. He begins with a list of precepts enunciated in a formal language with biblical intonations, approaching verse: "Be conscious of what happens to you from minute to minute... the event... misunderstood at the moment of being.... Write before sleep... in a book which can be taken with you as the past is taken with you, as the past takes you, which you will read with shame, remorse, and astonishment long after, in other circumstances. To keep a diary is an act of prayer, duplicating in your own meager power the gaze of the deity's blue eye upon you."[36] The "blue eye," the mediator between God and man, is the sky, so often in Schwartz's work the symbol of transcendent reality.

After an interchange with his disciples, who pose various problems, Dr. Bergen enunciates a second imperative: "Suppress nothing. Speak your whole mind fully and lucidly and without omission...."[37] A third and final imperative enjoins the examination of one's desires at the moment of feeling them—a monstrous precept which, if any man were capable of putting it into practice, would make life impossible. The doctor, then, represents consciousness in its most extreme form—consciousness developed to a point where it becomes pathological, the disease which afflicts so many of Schwartz's characters. In all of Dr.

Bergen's precepts the deity is presented as the supreme intellect, or consciousness. In this Platonic conception, God is the being in whom " 'Justice,' 'Truth,' 'Beauty,' are genuine and absolute."[38] He is also a terrifying deity, exacting and ever watchful. Little comfort is to be found in the bleak tenets of Dr. Bergen's belief.

A period of "Witness and Testimony" follows, in which each of the disciples tries to render an exact account of his concerns during the past week. Inevitably, they mention the dead Eleanor. The doctor declares that she killed herself because she "could not decide once for all what she wanted, except by examining her heart in the perspective of death." They play a record of her reading a poem she had written when she had believed that poetry offered a satisfying vocation. Like photographs and films, the record is a symbol of the recollected past; moreover, the subject of the poem is the relationship between the past and the present. The dead voice describes the peculiar playlike character life assumes when seen retrospectively,

> . . . when memory
> Holds up the past and dims the day,
> As in the future we shall see
> The present quickly passed away,
> Irrelevant to our belief,
> Misunderstood as every play. . . .

Hearing her voice, her lover Anthony reenters the living room. In torment he asks, "Who can distinguish now between the ghost/ And the actual, the living and the immortal?"[39] Like other characters of Schwartz's, he is baffled by the paradoxical survival in the present of what is past and dead.

The disciples now take turns in reciting their memories of Eleanor. They extol their idolatrously, upholding her life and her death as models for imitation. At this point, Dr. Newman interrupts the proceedings to accuse Dr. Bergen of propagating dangerous doctrines. In the argument that follows, Dr. Bergen supports the claims of intuition; and Dr. Newman insists upon the need to follow scientific method. Finally, to disprove Dr. Bergen's intuitive conviction that his daughter killed herself to be a "witness," the psychiatrist declares what he knows to be the truth: "She killed herself because she was in love with a married man." He reads a letter Eleanor wrote him, which says as much, and also mentions that she wants to have her father think that her suicide was "'in obedience to his religious belief.'"[40]

Maddened by this revelation, Dr. Bergen leaps to his death from the terrace; for he is determined to discover for himself whether there is a life beyond earthly existence, and willing to risk the abyss of total annihilation. His other daughter, Martha, follows him. Dr. Newman declaims, "Belief and knowledge consume the heart of man." Anthony continues: "Belief, knowledge, and desire—desire most of all." The play ends as Dr. Newman remarks, "Man destroys his own heart."[41]

IV Shenandoah

Like *Genesis*, *Shenandoah* (1941) is an ironic, meditative work that considers the individual in relation to the forces that shape his life, setting the personal past in a very broad historical and cultural context. The commentator on the play, Shenandoah as a grown man, speaks in verse that for the most part is mock Shakespearean. The play itself, in prose, centers around his mother's choice of his absurd name and culminates in the ceremony of his circumcision, the infliction of a symbolic wound which the name, itself a wound, or stigma, resembles. "The 'genteel' name Shenandoah," Politzer writes, "in stigmatizing the boy, forces him to become what his creator is: a solitary, an outsider, an exile from society, a poet."[42] Alfred Kazin says that Schwartz himself "saw in his mother's innocent cultural pretension a wound like circumcision, a sacramental duty to be different, a moral imperative to be unflinchingly serious and artistically responsible about the oddity—to him—of his first name."[43] Also, the forces that determine the choice of his name will work directly upon the child and in turn determine his personality.

The play opens with a prologue by the grown-up Shenandoah, who is spotlighted on a darkened stage. He compares the event of his naming with a number of famous trifles that changed history: the apple at Eden; the "trigger finger with the bitten nail" of the assassin at Sarajevo; and, with Pascal in mind, Cleopatra's nose, which would have affected the course of the whole world had it been longer. When the curtain rises, "a dining room/ In the lower middle class in 1914" is revealed. Its "period quality" has "the pathos/ Of any moment of time, seen in its pastness"; and the room is haunted by the shadowy presences of Israel and Europe. As Shenandoah speaks, his mother, Elsie Fish, enters with a neighbor, Edna Goldmark. In a bassinet she carries a baby, himself. She tells Edna that she is expecting a visit from her father-in-law, Jacob, who for some reason is disturbed, and also that she does not know the whereabouts of her husband. Shenandoah delivers a bitter speech against their marriage, "a stupid endless mistake."[44]

Jacob is upset, as he tells his daughter-in-law in the scene that follows, because the child is to be named after himself. It is considered unlucky, according to Jewish tradition, to use as a first name that of a living grandparent. Jacob's old-world values conflict with his awe at America. "I do not blame you for not knowing the beliefs of your religion and your people," he says. "You are only a woman, and in this great new America, anyone might forget everything but such wonderful things like tall buildings, subways, automobiles, and iceboxes."

Elsie agrees to change the name, even though it "has been announced on very expensive engraved cards." She has come to think that a new name is desirable in any case: "I want the boy to have an unusual name because he is going to be an unusual boy." How unusual she does not know. Absentmindedly handing the baby to the grown-up Shenandoah (there is, of course, no communication across the distance of time), she accompanies Jacob to the door while Shenandoah soliloquizes on "the world-wide powers" that will affect the child and "the vicious fate" that will make "an alien and freak" of him.[45]

The play resumes with another scene between Elsie and her neighbor, as they set about finding a name for the baby among the society notices of a newspaper. Mrs. Goldmark reads aloud while Mrs. Fish delivers judgment, dismissing name after name, commenting along the way on the privileges of the rich and expressing her desire to be among them. She takes a fancy to the name Delmore, but Mrs. Goldmark obliviously reads on. At length, she comes to an announcement that certain society people have an estate in the Shenandoah Valley. Mrs. Fish eagerly accepts the name as the baby howls and the commentator laments. The women leave the stage, and once more Shenandoah takes the baby in his arms.

There follows a soliloquy by Shenandoah on naming. The name reflects the deepest wishes of the parents for the child. It may be vile "in order to outwit the evil powers." It may be the name of an event occurring at the time of his birth. "This child by that rule would thus be named/ 'The First World War'—" Or a child may take the name of his father: ". . . the wish is clear/ All men would live forever—" Or he may be named after a place, "tacit/ Admission of the part the *milieu* plays," or after professions or saints. God Himself is "The Nameless" to Jews, being "the anonymous Father of all hearts." Shenandoah concludes that the child should have the right to choose his own name when he is old enough.[46]

In the next scene, the family, gathered for the circumcision ceremony, is awaiting the arrival of the rabbi. Also present are two business acquaintances of the father who vie with each other for the privilege of being the child's godfather. The father tells them that this is to be granted to Elsie's brother Nathan, a promising young doctor. When Nathan arrives and learns the proposed name, he protests violently: "The boy will be handicapped as if he had a clubfoot."[47] Nathan is respected by the family, but in this instance the father overrules his educated good sense. Angry, he leaves the room; and the rest of the family follows, quarreling, leaving Shenandoah alone once again with the baby, to whom he describes the forces that are at work:

> To bring about the person of your name:
> Europe! America! the fear of death!
> Belief and half-belief in Zion's word!
> The order of a community in which
> The lower middle class looks up or gapes
> And strives to imitate the sick élite
> In thought, in emptiness, in luxury;
> Also the foreigner whose foreign-ness
> Names his son native, speaking broken English—[48]

Shenandoah cites the men who will be the child's spiritual masters when he grows older, the great contemporary writers, all of whom suffer exile in one form or another, incapable of

changing the course of history yet heroically bearing witness.
These lines, referred to in the fourth section of Chapter 3, are
without doubt Schwartz's most eloquent homage to the world
of culture that he chose, as opposed to the family past that was
his by birth.

Still quarreling about the name, the family reenters, and soon
afterward the rabbi, Dr. Adamson, arrives. Shenandoah hopes
that, as the inheritor of ancient wisdom, he may give good and
effective advice; but the rabbi is too conciliatory, and his mild
efforts to make peace are futile. Elsie then suggests that her
husband call his lawyer, Kelly, for advice, whereupon Shenandoah remarks, "She seeks the Gentile world, the Gentile voice!/
The ancient wisdom is far from enough,/ Far from enough her
husband's cleverness—" Insulted, Dr. Adamson threatens to
leave, suggesting that Kelly perform the rite of circumcision. The
father cynically replies, ". . . it is always best to hear what
everyone has to say. *After all, this child is going to live in a
world of Kellys!*" The rabbi humbly resigns himself: "The
modern world is what it is."

The father calls Kelly, who tells him in the course of a wise-
cracking conversation that the name Shenandoah is a good one.
"*He guarantees that it is a good name!*" the father exults. But
the adult Shenandoah suspects a malice in the approval of the
Irish Catholic that dooms him as much as the ignorance of
his family. The father and Nathan make up (Shenandoah, for-
getting the distance of time like the narrator of "In Dreams
Begin Responsibilities," tries to shake his hand "across the
years" for having tried to help); and all the men in the party
go into the next room for the ceremony, bringing the baby.
Shenandoah comments: "How profound/ Are all these ancient
rites: for with a wound/ —What better sign exists—the child is
made/ A Jew forever!" For the Jew is "an heir to lasting pain."
He mentions Hitler, and describes the fate of the Jews to be
one of "wandering and alienation."[49]

From the next room comes the voice of the rabbi as he intones
the rite, and then the cry of the baby, whereupon Shenandoah
begins his last speech: "Silent, O child, for if a knife can make
you cry,/ What will you do when you know that you must
die?/ When the mind howls with the body, *I am I*?" Naming,
which symbolizes the assumption of identity, is accompanied by

a wound, which anticipates death; and to know that one is an individual (*"I am I"* will recall the same tautology at the end of "A Young Child and His Pregnant Mother") is to know that one must die. The play draws to a close as Shenandoah foresees "the horrors of modern life," which the child must face, and the persecution of his people. There is only one consolation—that of understanding, of giving form to experience, of bearing witness, whereby "transient release is known, in the darkened theater's plays...."[50]

V Genesis

This fragment of fictional autobiography, *Genesis* (1943), Schwartz's longest work, brings its hero, Hershey Green, to his fourteenth year. It also contains episodes of family history, such as the courtship of his father and mother, which recalls "In Dreams Begin Responsibilities." It places the lives of Hershey's paternal grandparents, Noah and Hannah Green, against the historical background of the war between Russia and Turkey in 1878, and tells of his father's emigration to America. It narrates the adventures of his mother's family as well: how her father, Noah Newman, married Leah, the daughter of a rich merchant; how he went to America alone, to be followed later by the rest of his family.

The story is mostly about Hershey, a "New York boy" growing up in "Europe's last capital," who is the perceptive and sensitive child of a failed marriage. In the shadow of his parents, he seeks the meaning of his life, becoming aware of a world of beauty as represented by the voice of Galli-Curci; of religious mysteries, sex, and the inexplicable stigma of being Jewish. F. O. Matthiesen calls *Genesis* a *Bildungsroman*—a work belonging to the genre of fiction that portrays the development and education of the hero, such as Thomas Mann's *Buddenbrooks*, Marcel Proust's *Swann's Way*, and James Joyce's *Portrait of the Artist as a Young Man.*[51]

Hershey tells his story to several ghosts who visit him one night in his bedroom. They are not named, but they are probably the spirits of famous men, like those in *Coriolanus and His Mother.* In his preface, Schwartz compares them to "the chorus in Greek drama."[52] They provide, as Matthiesen says, "great

density of reference";[53] for their purpose is to universalize the
life of the hero by drawing upon several areas of knowledge,
including history, myth, literature, philosophy, and psychology.
They also refer to such popular sources as motion pictures and
comic strips. Being ghosts, they can survey the hero's life from
an absolute vantage point, which R. P. Blackmur calls "the
lasting condition of expressive death."[54]

The ghostly witnesses are bitterly aware of the irony that
inheres in their position—for all their knowledge, they are
ineffectual commentators on an unalterable and often pathetically
comic past, like Schwartz's other observers:

> "Psychologize, young man, all we do is
> Psychologize, thinking of Might-Have-Been,
> Lights of our former lives mistakes and stakes,
> Powerless, overwhelmed by consciousness,
> Anguished for those who do not know their lives,"
> Sang one ghost, passionate and piteous. . . .[55]

In contrast to the ghosts with their omniscience, the living
are blind in their present. On the one hand, there is the helplessness of objective knowledge; on the other, the helplessness
of ignorant, subjective experience:

> "We from our death must laugh about the living,
> Just as the living, looking back, laugh too,
> At the past's pastness, period quality:
> The dresses seem ridiculous, that brummel
> Tipping his bowler hat is certainly
> Ridiculous! The dead see this, when you are dead
> You too will laugh about the living ones. . . ."[56]

In their "lasting condition of expressive death" the ghosts
of *Genesis* embody absolutely the hopeless, irreconcilable conflict between experience and consciousness. With their lamenting,
ironic voices, they represent a state of mind to which the past,
though forever lost, remains poignantly alive, like the images
on the silent screen in the darkness of the movie theater, which
so engross the hero of "In Dreams Begin Responsibilities" that
he forgets, at times, that they are untouchable shadows and
cries out to them.

The life of Hershey Green is representatively human. Schwartz sees the individual, the self or ego, as acted upon by the forces of the past and as upset by the impingements of chance, by contingent events; yet he considers the possibility that freedom may nevertheless exist. One view of the past is reminiscent of poems such as "The Ballad of the Children of the Czar," "Someone is Harshly Coughing as Before," and "In the Naked Bed, in Plato's Cave." The past recurs endlessly, it resumes in the life of each new individual; and with this view the putative freedom and uniqueness of the individual must be reconciled. As a ghost declares toward the end of *Genesis*,

> "The history of Life repeats its endless circle, over and
> over and over again,
> In the new boy, in the new city, in the time forever
> new, forever old,
> —All of the famous characters are glimpsed again,
> All the well-known events; yet something new,
> Unique, undying, free, blessèd or damned!"[57]

Many of Schwartz's references, as he describes the "endless circle," are to the Jewish past. The names of several of the characters of *Genesis* are from the Old Testament. In some cases, it is easy to draw parallels to ancient prototypes: Hershey's mother is Eva; a ne'er-do-well uncle, Ishmael; and Noah is the name of both of his grandfathers. Other characters with biblical names—Hannah, Benjamin, Leah—do not particularly resemble their namesakes. Of course, the name of the work itself is biblical.

The past of Israel is comprehended by the general human past. The growing boy is likened to many historical, mythical, and literary figures. When he is disgraced in class, he relives a timeless moment: "Exiled, humiliated, persecuted, Coriolanus, Joseph, and Caesar, the child resumes history, each enacts all that has been."[58]

Similar references illustrate primordial human experiences: " 'In each, all natural being once more lives!/ The subtile [*sic*] serpent which the apple brought/ To Mamma and Papa, starting all!' "[59] And a bit later: " 'Eden, image of many complex thoughts/ About beginning, hangs just like a picture/ In many living rooms in the Western World. . . .' "[60]

Typically, the life of the individual is set against the wider background of impersonal events and contemporary world history whose forces, or "causes," affect his personal, private life:

"How clearly now, we see, young man, *too late*,
Those mighty world-wide thoughtless causes which
Suddenly shake a dining room so much,
Shaking the dining room where a private man
Sits drinking tea with family and friends
And eating fish, swallows a bone and chokes!
Killed by the quake prepared how many years
Motiveless in the turning globe's round shelves—"[61]

These numerous "thoughtless causes" are referred to throughout *Genesis* as "deities" or "divinities":

"Giant, phenomenal, and purposeless,
How the divinities, America,
Europe, Capitalismus, others too,
Move through the life of this Atlantic Jew!"[62]

Among the other "causes" are nature, school ("the school divinity"), and New York City, "Europe's last capital." There are also the psychological divinities, Freud's "Pleasure-Principle," the "Id," and the "Super-Ego." Over all of them rules time: "'No one of all the deities that then/ Presided over the little tired boy/ Free of that first dominion, Time....' "[63]

The ghosts are fascinated by chance as well as by deterministic forces, and they like to speculate about alternatives to what has actually happened. As in "In Dreams Begin Responsibilities," the courtship of the hero's parents arouses horrified fascination, for it is the cast of the dice that will decide his existence:

"My thoughts are like a cold and driving rain
Seen in November from the windowpane,"
One ghost said then, "Necessity is there:
Yet by an accident it all begins!
—How, in the time of courtship, trembles
(As when the ball races the roulette wheel
And seems and then seems not about to stop
On the best hope) wondrous Might-Not-Have-Been!

> —This thought is an abyss, when understood!
> I see this marriage hanging from a ledge
> Fifty-five floors above the city street."[64]

The narrator of the story, watching his parents, feels "like one who looks down on the avenue from the 50th story of a building."[65] Thought of past contingencies produces vertigo and nausea.

Nevertheless, in spite of everything that might seem to deny it, "'Freedom remains amid necessity .... Perhaps/ The pure event leaps from the infinite cave,/ Strange child without known father, like a star!'"[66] It is in keeping with Schwartz's associations that the "pure event" should be compared to a child, a new individual, at the moment of birth.

Although *Genesis* has by no means a religious orientation—the forces that shape the child are completely of this world—the protagonist and his companions nevertheless refer often to a hypothetical God; and Hershey has visions of a transcendent realm beyond the banalities of his existence. While he has no positive commitment to belief of any kind, he still longs for a purity and perfection that will somehow set to rights the sad disorder he sees on every side; he yearns for an impossible atonement.

The theatrical metaphor that pervades *Genesis* and the other works of this chapter serves to describe the relationship of God Himself to His creation. "'Everything happens in the mind of God,'" cries a ghost. "'This is the play it is, ever since Eden!'" This idea—that God is the supreme spectator of His own play, the world—enthralls Hershey:

> "Everything happens in the mind of God?
> —This news is thrilling and I hope it true!
> It is like looking at the sky's round blue,
> Blue within blue within blue endlessly.
> And does the angel Gabriel know it too?
> All the scenes of my life?
> My intimate emotions?"[67]

The image of the blue sky in this context is familiar; and that other powerful image for transcendence, the snow, appears throughout *Genesis*. As it will be recalled from the third section of Chapter 3, *Genesis* reveals the full range of Schwartz's obsession with snow, from immediate delight at the actual humble miracle, with its suggestions of desired oblivion, to its association with a state of total, blissful awareness on the other side of death. The following passage incorporates, at the end, lines quoted earlier:

> "O, when the snow falls, he forgives all shame,
> Forgets the turning world and every hope,
> And every memory of guilt and pain,
> He seeks no future and regrets no past,
> Satisfied by the fat white pieces' fall—
>
> "As one is satisfied, playing a game!
> A game which makes activity pure joy,
> Being itself Being itself, and more
> Than striving for the absent future end—
> Thus perhaps blessed souls, risen at last
> To full eternity, must gaze upon
> The infinite light that makes the universe,
> And know a pleasure perfect and serene!"[68]

This passage brings together the two aspects of snow discussed earlier—its association with death (Heaven being the state one must die to enter), and its association, through comparison with light, with creation and generation. As has been noted, light replaces snow in Schwartz's last poems, where it comes to symbolize "summer knowledge." The change is anticipated in *Genesis*, and in a passage, moreover, that immediately follows the description of snow as "the death of the colored world."[69] The sight of it arouses in the hero a desire for blissful oblivion, yet paradoxically a ghost describes his happiness with images of "the colored world" in the fullness of life. Hershey is

> "Happy as some in May, in the May morning
> When sunlight stamps gold coins on the blazed gaze,
> And on the river does the diamond dance. . . ."

There follows only a line later a hymn to the sun:

> "O sun of nature! source of all the forces,
> All blooms, all snakes, and Botticelli's views

Of both of these, and Nature as a dance:
(Light is the heroine of every picture—)"[70]

Genesis, while it is the most elaborate statement of Schwartz's earlier themes, also looks forward to work to come, in which light, and what it represents, will in fact be the "heroine."

Now one must ask whether the poet has fulfilled the purpose he expresses in his preface to *Genesis:* to write in his time and for his time a long, philosophical poem informed by beliefs and values that give universal and enduring relevance to the facts of individual experience. He speaks of the good fortune of writers who "live in an age when their beliefs and values are embodied in great institutions and in the way of life of many human beings. These authors do not have to bring in their beliefs and values from the outside. . . ." The present, however, "is a time of much variety of belief . . . . No author can assume a community of ideas and values between himself and his audience." Now he touches upon his own problem in writing *Genesis:* "Hence he must bring in his ideas and values openly and clearly."[71]

The question is, how can the writer do this without thereby betraying the spirit of poetry with intellectual abstraction? Though the ghosts in *Genesis* are meant to dramatize attitudes toward experience rather than promote philosophical speculation as an end in itself or serve as mouthpieces for doctrines to which the poet positively adheres, Schwartz's use of ideas is still for the most part inimical to poetry; and his method of universalizing particulars by means of innumerable references is mechanical and repetitious. Poems are not made of ideas. Whatever assertions a poet may make, and upon whatever level of intellectual abstraction, his sensibility must inform his poem with an interpretation of reality that is deeper than any formulation or assertion of the intellect alone.

Schwartz himself says as much in his essay, "Poetry and Belief in Thomas Hardy." Speaking of Hardy's "The Oxen," in which the poet longs to believe in a country legend that farm animals kneel down in their stalls in homage to Christ on Christmas Eve, Schwartz asserts the paradox that the poet's very disbelief was a form of belief and that the success of "The Oxen" depends upon a tension between a traditional outlook and modern doctrines that were more congenial to Hardy's intellect. "The belief in this poem is of course the disbelief in the truth of Christianity. The emotion is the wish that it were true."

This emotion "depends upon a very full sense of what the belief in Christianity amounted to . . . . It is Hardy's sensibility as the son of his fathers which makes possible his realization of the specific scene and story; this sensibility itself was the product of definite beliefs . . . . But for the whole poem to be written, it was necessary that what Hardy's sensibility made him conscious of should be held against the scientific view which his intellect accepted. Both must enter the poem."[72] On the other hand, "when Hardy states his intellectual beliefs directly his poem often fails. . . ." Hardy "needs his sensibility; but his sensibility works only when the objects proper to it are in view. When it is required to function in a cosmological scene, it can only produce weak and incommensurate figures. It is possible for the poet to make poetry by the direct statement of his beliefs, but it is not possible for such a poet as Hardy."[73] Nor is it possible for such a poet as Delmore Schwartz. One can only wish that he had taken his own advice.

The function of Hardy's belief—or disbelief—"was to generalize his experience into something neither merely particular, which is the historian's concern, nor merely general, which is the philosopher's; but into symbols which possess the qualitative richness . . . of any particular thing and yet have the generality which makes them significant beyond their moment of existence, or the passing context in which they are located."[74]

Schwartz's own "sensibility" was uninformed by any system of traditional belief; yet when he allows it to function untrammeled by abstraction, it can give a dimension to particular experiences that is beyond the power of any amount of intellectual effort, specifically the effort to universalize by means of excessive references to myth, history, literature and the rest. The successful verse passages in *Genesis* occur precisely when he forgets the intellectual apparatus he has devised, as in this evocation of a desolate night in New York:

> "The autos move with goggle eyes dead-white
> And in the glasses of the wet streets draw

Slanting pillar-like rays which slide with them,
The while the rain on roofs makes cracks of sounds,
The driving autumn rain in the sick city!
—This is the image of the city life—"[75]

Confronting the city directly, the poet presents an "image of the city life" in which the observed particulars convey an impression of New York as a place of mechanical desolation, destructive to life. The "autos" in this passage, and the "pillar-like rays which slide with them" recall "the moving street on which the autos slide" in "Someone Is Harshly Coughing as Before," and "the sliding auto's catastrophe" in "O City, City."

"As it is," says Matthiesen, having commented on the flatness of so much of the verse in *Genesis,* "we are faced with the anomaly that the most lyrical passages of the book are expressed in prose."[76] This flatness of the verse results not only from excessive abstraction but also from the unbroken metrical pattern, iambic pentameter. In his later work Schwartz struggled to escape from this rigidity into a freer form, as have other poets of his generation, including Robert Lowell and John Berryman. It should be noted, if only in passing, that the innovations of Ezra Pound, William Carlos Williams, and T. S. Eliot had little effect on Schwartz's prosody, however much he admired them, especially the last. The prose of *Genesis* offers a relief from convention. Also, the poet evidently did not feel the need to burden his prose with the abstract speculations that the verse form generated, in part, perhaps, because of its associations with epic solemnity.

Genesis, to conclude, is not a neglected masterpiece. If it has interest, it is because of the problems it confronts and the questions it raises, and because it relates to an aspect of Schwartz's own critical theory which he unfortunately did not practice in the poem itself. Formally, *Genesis* dramatizes the confrontation of experience by the removed, analytic mind; and it brings into play all of the ironies inherent in this confrontation, developing to the farthest extent the theatrical relationship that appears in one form or another in the works discussed in this chapter.

CHAPTER 6

The World Is a Wedding

F OUR of the seven stories of the collection *The World Is a Wedding* (1948)—"America! America!," "New Year's Eve," "The Child Is the Meaning of This Life," and "The World Is a Wedding"—are closer to traditional realistic fiction than the remaining three, discussed earlier—"A Bitter Farce," an anecdote, "The Statues," a parable, and "In Dreams Begin Responsibilities," a fantasy. Writing in these four stories without excessive philosophical commentary from the standpoint of a detached and ironic observer, Schwartz avoids the graceless abstraction that disfigures *Genesis*. Though far less ambitious than his labored attempt to forge a personal epic, the stories are more faithful than the poem to the world they depict and are more informed by Schwartz's awareness of it, which he projects with a style of casual power.[1] It may even be that he succeeded in these stories precisely because he did not feel compelled to try so hard to construct a literary monument.

All four stories first appeared in the *Partisan Review* during the 1940's, and all but one of them, "New Year's Eve," which describes the malaise and helplessness of intellectuals just before the outbreak of World War II, center in one way or another around the Depression of the preceding decade, which gave the lie to the aspirations of their characters. In "America! America!," the United States is described as "the land of promise," an epithet that recalls not only the Jewish dream of salvation but also that of most Americans, especially immigrants. The primary mood of Schwartz's characters is one of disillusionment, which casts its shadow back over the past, so that all striving seems pathetic, sometimes comically so, in retrospect, a futile sacrifice. The members of the older generation, with their "grotesque Americanism and corrupted Judaism,"[2] as Politzer has aptly remarked, have disowned the past without having really found themselves as Americans; and their children, for the most part embittered intellectuals, laugh at them.

The stories were warmly praised when the collection first appeared, as well as in later reevaluations. With his fiction uppermost in mind, Irving Howe has said that "Schwartz's best work brought one to the very edge of the absurd, and there, almost as if ironic distance were a perquisite for affection, one could find a certain half-peace in contemplating the world of one's youth."[3]

While these stories are especially meaningful for Jewish readers who were growing up during the years in which they are set, they should also appeal to readers of whatever age or background who are opposed to some of the manifest purposes and values of modern life; who have tried, as Schwartz himself tried, to comprehend a world that has little comprehension of itself; and who feel, as Schwartz himself felt, that they both belong to that world and live isolated from it. At their farthest reach, the best of the stories embrace the suffering that art tries to heal with whatever power it properly has to do so.

I "America! America!"

"America! America!" describes the rise and fall of the Baumanns, who are friends of the parents of Shenandoah Fish, and the poet's feelings of alienation from their world, which are revealed as he listens to his mother's ironic account of their prosperity and later misery. The story ends with Shenandoah's realization that he is, as a writer, the very product of this world. It receives a philosophical emphasis when he questions whether it is possible really to know oneself or others. Despairingly, he concludes that it is not: one can never see others as they see themselves, nor can one see oneself as others do.

Mr. Baumann, a Russian immigrant who established a successful insurance business early in the century, has, like his family and friends, an unbounded faith in America:

When the first plane flew, when elevators became common, when the new subway was built, some newspaper reader in the Baumann

Dexter Library
Northland College
Ashland, Wisconsin 54806

household would raise his head, announce the wonder, and exclaim:
"You see: America!"

When the toilet-bowl flushed like Niagara, when a suburban
homeowner killed his wife and children, and when a Jew was made
a member of President Theodore Roosevelt's cabinet, the excited
exclamation was:

"America! America!"[4]

Though the Baumanns do not become rich, they are happy
with their lot; for they believe that they have truly come to
the Promised Land; and they cherish the American dream of
progress. However, they still keep a vestige of old-world values;
and they have a Jewish respect, if a misdirected one, for learning. Mrs. Baumann, for example, admires Bergson and Freud.
She "relished their fame to the point of making out a misleading
and mistaken version of their doctrines...."[5] The Baumanns
are rather endearing in spite of their fatuous materialism.
Grateful for their prosperity, they generously receive into their
home "the human beings who have gone from the community
life of the old country and foundered amid the immense alienation of metropolitan life."[6]

Yet everything goes wrong for them. Mr. Baumann's hopes
have no issue. Both of his sons, Dick and Sidney, are failures;
in part, because they never had the incentive of poverty that
moved their parents; in part, because the very qualities that
helped their father to succeed—gregariousness and *savoir-vivre*,
assets for him in acquiring clients—work against them. The failure of the sons reveals the inability of the older generation to
transmit such values as they possess. The Depression, which
Sidney uses to justify his failure, puts an end to all their hopes.

This is the story that Shenandoah's mother tells him in her
kitchen, where he is sitting out the Depression in his bathrobe,
as it were. She speaks with ironic inflections; and as he listens,
silently adding ironic commentary of his own, he reflects upon
his own maladjustment in the uncomprehending, middle-class
world that the Baumanns represent. At first, he feels totally
apart from it: "He reflected upon his separation from these
people, and he felt that in every sense he was removed from
them by thousands of miles, or by a generation, or by the Atlantic Ocean." He feels that he is a "monster," and that they ought
to be "his genuine relatives and friends." But as he listens, he

realizes that he is "wrong to suppose that the separation, the contempt, and the gulf had nothing to do with his work; perhaps, on the contrary, it was the center; or perhaps it was the starting-point and compelled the innermost motion of the work to be flight, or criticism, or denial, or rejection."[7]

He discovers that he is close to the world of the Baumanns in a more direct way: he has been as deceived and defeated in his own hopes as an artist as they have been in their dreams of material success. "His separation was actual enough, but there existed also an unbreakable unity. As the air was full of the radio's unseen voices, so the life he breathed was full of these lives and the age in which they had acted and suffered." They are all—the Baumanns, their friends, and Shenandoah himself—victims of the historical moment and of a fatality that runs counter to human aspirations and goals.

He also realizes that the Baumanns seem ridiculous because he sees them from the outside and in retrospect. Now he knows that he himself, seen in retrospect, will seem as comic and foolish as they. "He felt that the contemptuous mood which had governed him as he listened was really self-contempt and ignorance. He thought that his own life invited the same irony." On the other hand, he realizes, "How different it might seem if he had been able to see these lives from the inside, looking out." Without the sad irony of retrospect, he would have known them subjectively and in their own present.

He comes to a bitter conclusion. Alone in his room he confronts himself in his mirror; and typical of a hero of Schwartz's, he feels "the curious omniscience gained in looking at old photographs where the posing faces and the old-fashioned clothes and the moment itself seem ridiculous, ignorant, and unaware of the period quality which is truly there, and the subsequent revelation of waste and failure." He recalls his mother's final observation in concluding the Baumann family saga, that "some human beings seemed to be ruined by their best qualities"; and he accepts this generalization as one that describes "the fate of all human beings and his own fate." He arrives at a despairing awareness of human limitations: " 'No one truly exists in the real world because no one knows all that he is to other human beings, all that they say behind his back, and all the foolishness which the future will bring him.' "[8]

II "New Year's Eve"

The story "New Year's Eve" again comments upon the presumed inability of "human beings" to understand one another. Its main characters are intellectuals who, because of mistrust of themselves and their companions, use their minds as instruments of torture. The story culminates in a dismal New Year's Eve party that they attend in order to relieve their anxiety over the imminence of "the profound holiday," which "is full of pain because it is both an ending and a beginning."[9] The year about to begin is 1938, "the infamous year of the Munich Pact."[10] Among the celebrants are Shenandoah Fish, "promising young author"; his fiancée, Wilhelmina Gold; a male friend of his own age, Nicholas O'Neil; three married couples; and an unwanted, self-invited guest, Leon Berg, who brings the story to its crisis.

Some of the characters are first seen during the rainy, dreary afternoon preceding the party, when the narrator follows them about the impersonal city. Shenandoah, hoping for words of praise for a recently published work, drops in at the office of his publisher, Grant Landis, who is giving the party. Grant invites Shenandoah and his friends, to the distaste of his partner Arthur Harris, who tells him when the young man has left: " 'There is enough alienation in modern life without installing it in the living room.' " Shenandoah notices Arthur's annoyance, but he misunderstands it, thinking that his work is under attack.

"And as they argued and as they irritated each other" during the afternoon, "elsewhere in other boxes of the great city old conflicts were renewed and new ones quickly engendered."[11] Grant's wife Martha quarrels with her mother-in-law on the phone, Shenandoah and Nicholas quarrel about a poem, and Grant is angry with his mother for having interfered in his married life. Meanwhile, Wilhelmina Gold and her mother quarrel about Shenandoah, who does not answer to Mrs. Gold's idea of a suitable match for her daughter.

When the evening comes, Shenandoah and Nicholas are reluctant to go to the party. Nevertheless, they set out to meet Wilhelmina, as if they had no choice, no will. They all go to Grant's apartment, only to be told that the party will take place at Arthur's house; for Arthur thinks he has a cold and wants to stay home. With Grant and his wife are another couple, Oliver and Delia Jones. Oliver, a writer, is mistrustful of his talent; as a result, he is dishonest and suspects others of harboring the worst intentions. Delia, whom Oliver does not love, is an attractive woman; but like her husband, she is utterly unsure of herself. She makes half-hearted attempts to have love affairs with other men, with Oliver's encouragement.

The party is disappointing, and none of the guests really wants to be there. Shenandoah, who unwittingly awakens Oliver's self-doubts and is attacked, withdraws into himself, feeling self-pity. Gradually, the story focuses upon Delia, who feels obliged to make an effort to seduce some man. Because she has never had success, she imagines that she is unattractive: "She did not understand that it was not a question of a defect in her, but of the difficulty of direct communication in modern life. . . ."[12]

As the evening advances, an alcoholic feeling of well-being and intimacy settles over the guests; and they indulge in much gossip at the expense of those not present. To torment himself and others with a reminder of forgotten ideals, Oliver reads aloud from Edmund Wilson's *Axel's Castle* a passage describing the devotion of a character in Proust to the vocation of art. He immediately denounces Proust, and Shenandoah remarks to himself, " 'His overworked conscience has just enjoyed some relief by spitting itself in the face.' "[13] This incident marks the end of the conviviality.

When Leon Berg, who is to be this forlorn party's catalyst, phones and invites himself, he inspires a fresh rage of malice among the guests. On the way to the party, Leon out of spite drops in on an acquaintance, "a minor poet," who fears him because he discounts all writers, "including Shakespeare." He malevolently insists that "all modern poets were worthless because they did not have the effect upon History of John L. Lewis and Bing Crosby. . . ." As he leaves, he remarks misanthropically that "there would be no new world war because so many human beings expected a war and so many human beings had never been right about anything."[14]

At the party, Delia, now thoroughly drunk, is flirting with the men one by one, asking, " 'Who are you?' " When Leon enters, she greets him with the same question. When, suspecting hos-

tility, he flings it angrily back at her, " 'Who are *you*?,' " she
is overcome. "No one knew if Delia's consternation was the
consequence of Leon's triumphant and leering face, or the
result of her actually being unable to think of who she was."[15]
In her distress, she represents the self-estrangement of everyone
at the party. Her husband takes her into one of the bedrooms,
where she breaks down and attacks him hysterically, to be com-
forted by Arthur's wife.

The rest of the guests have forgotten to observe the coming
of the new year, though the radio is playing "that they might
know the exact moment of passage and unbearable beauty."
They go to the window and see that snow has fallen, "the most
beautiful of all the illusions of the natural world." No one
knows that this year will be the last year of peace, "but everyone knew that soon there would be a new world war because
only a few unimportant or powerless people believed in God
or in the necessity of a just society sufficiently to be willing to
give anything dear for it." Shenandoah is "already locked in
what was soon to be a post-Munich sensibility: complete hope-
lessness of perception and feeling."

He vainly invokes "some other world" where people will live
by laws revealed to them by "the examination of consciousness."[16] Like Dr. Bergen, he believes that this exercise can
lead to salvation. But what the characters of the story lack is
love. Their "consciousness" is ruinous and only serves to widen
the rift between themselves and the world. The story ends with
Wilhelmina's refusal to marry Shenandoah and have children.
Mockingly, Nicholas repeats Delia's forlorn question, with Leon's
emphasis, " 'Who are *you*?' "[17] This question none of these characters would be able to answer.

III   "The Child Is the Meaning of This Life"

"The Child Is the Meaning of This Life" resembles "America!
America!" in being a family chronicle; but it differs from it in
that it does not depict the conflict of intellectual offspring with
their environment. Mostly without philosophical commentary,
this story focuses almost entirely upon character and upon the
conversations and small actions that reveal it. A tone of under-
statement pervades the story, and the ironic effect is heightened

by the reader's awareness that the narrator is holding in abeyance a shrewd and powerful wit.

With one exception, its characters are entirely blind to any values beyond the conventional. The story is a portrayal of life without faith, imagination, or meaningful work. But Schwartz's sympathy is such that one finds in the end something more than mere negation. "The Child Is the Meaning of This Life" is, for all its bleakness, about the possibility of survival beyond the defeat of expectations, about the possibility of love, which can strike a spark in desperate situations.

The main character of the story is Ruth Hart, a widow whose husband has died of overwork, from trying too hard for business success. Ruth is left with four growing children, Rebecca, Sarah, Leonard, and the youngest child, Samuel (later renamed Seymour for the sake of refinement). The story is about her stoic endurance and the development of her children, who never stray far from her; but Samuel occupies the center of the stage for the most part. In terms of his relationship to the others, and to Ruth in particular, the story proceeds, bringing in the untimely death of Leonard, a medical student, Sarah's unhappy marriage, and Rebecca's self-sacrifice, fear of spinsterhood, and her own eventual marriage, also unhappy. The story also traces the growth of Sarah's own children, Nancy and Jasper, especially his slow rise to maturity and his professional success as a lawyer. Intelligent and idealistic, he is Samuel's opposite in every respect. Toward the end of the story, he displaces Samuel as the center of narrative attention. Ruth, too, emerges from the background, and the last sight of her is through her grandson's eyes.

Samuel, whose destiny in life is to become a bookie, is spoiled, selfish, and without ambition. "I am not the successful type,"[18] he says of himself. "I've been a failure all my life." He indolently relishes his own verdict. One of his friends remarks, "Samuel looks just like a big baby."[19] He prefers the company of Jasper and Nancy, both of whom he bullies mercilessly, to that of adults, from whom he hides in his room. Naïvely disreputable, he steals money to gamble with, always believing that he will win and be able to repay it. His only good trait, itself arising from his dependency, is his love for Ruth, whose possible death he cannot face.

Samuel exemplifies the mediocrity, the lack of idealism of his milieu, whose values, such as they are, he reflects negatively. The pursuit of success has a direct bearing upon his own passivity and futility and his isolation in a household of women. He has no masculine examples to follow, for both his father and brother have died of the strain of overwork; and Sarah's husband, Michael, neglects his family in part for the sake of his ambition to get ahead in business. As a failure, Samuel is the opposite of Michael; but he admires his arrogant brother-in-law, who embodies the ideal of a success that Samuel has no incentive to try for. His admiration is a commentary upon the hollowness of Michael's way of life. When the Depression comes, the paper fortune of Michael vanishes, the hollowness is exposed, and Samuel, in his perdurable futility, is seen as having pointed the direction in which, all along, this way of life was tending.

Samuel's sisters, Rebecca and Sarah, have minor roles in the story; and their purpose in part is to set off Samuel's relationship to Ruth. Both girls are subordinate to him in his mother's eyes, especially the self-sacrificing Rebecca. "It was for Samuel and not for Rebecca that his mother went down to the store in the cold early mornings of winter to get fresh rolls and coffee cake."[20] Rebecca is expected to put away money for a dowry and at the same time repay money Samuel steals for gambling. Her fate is to marry, out of fear of spinsterhood, the ridiculous James Mannheim, an incompetent dentist and, like Samuel, a figure of masculine weakness. While Rebecca is resigned, Sarah is stubborn and hard in her dealings with her family and with the world at large; and she detests Samuel. Still, though she is utterly without softness and warmth, she too is a victim—of herself. With her penuriousness and obstinacy, she alienates Michael. Her groundless hope that he will return to her adds yet another stroke to this portrayal of human futility and delusion.

Ruth alone, the stable center of the family, has dignity and wisdom, apart from Jasper, who represents the future. One becomes aware of her personality largely in terms of her influence upon the others, but her portrait sharpens toward the end of the story. At a surprise party for her seventy-fifth birthday there are intimations of a life apart from her immediate family: ". . . a friend of the family who had known Ruth when her first child was born made a short speech in which she had said that of all the human beings she had known, and she had known many, Ruth was the kindest, the most generous, the most devoted, and the least selfish."[21]

Finally, the reader sees her through the eyes of Jasper, who is also now in the foreground of the story. She is in a hospital, recovering from a heart attack: "As he entered the hospital room, Jasper saw that his grandmother was exchanging witticisms with the old ladies who were patients. She was overwhelmed to see him and she began to cry while Jasper felt a paralysis of face, so strong was the shock at how shrunken and yellow his grandmother looked."

This rare physical description brings Ruth into final focus. In her shrunkenness, one sees the years that have passed, becoming fully aware of the long range of time covered by this relatively brief story. Also, as at the surprise party, one sees Ruth in a social context, apart from the members of her family. She assures her grandson, " 'I am going to live for a long time.' "[22] They discuss the future and her hopes for his marriage; and, as if to ensure her survival in some fashion, he tells her that his wife must be like her.

Before this encounter Jasper muses over his childhood and the influences that have shaped him, considering the power of the past and the possibilities of the future. Janus-faced, like Schwartz's other characters, he asks, "What was the freedom to which the adult human being rose in the morning, if each act was held back or inspired by the overpowering ghost of a little child? This freedom seemed to Jasper like the freedom, dangerous, dark, and far-off, to become the father of new children without knowing at all what would become of them. . . ."[23] As Jasper is leaving the hospital after his visit, he tells himself: " 'The child is the mystery of this life. And the child is the meaning of this life.' " The story ends as a stranger asks him if he has a light. " 'No, I have no light,' " he answers, with a symbolic emphasis.[24]

IV   "The World Is a Wedding"

The longest story of the group, "The World Is a Wedding" portrays the attitudes of intellectuals who came to maturity during the Depression. Like the others, it offers little physical description, and factual details of any kind are minimal. It shows the farthest development of Schwartz's method of evoking character and mood by means of conversation and by modulations of the narrator's tone of voice. The young people of the story, all of them literate and given to analysis of themselves and one another, indulge in a continual play of language. Their personalities, in which co-exist idealism and cynicism, romantic expectation and disillusionment, perceptivity and obtuseness, offer endless possibilities for the exercise of their own ironic point of view and that of the effaced narrator who stands behind them all.

Unable or unwilling to act, the characters of this story resort to words. "They use up their lives in commenting on life," Politzer remarks. "They are not persons but grotesque abbreviations of living people in whom the sparks of vitality are extinguished."[25] The very structure of "The World Is a Wedding" is determined by this emphasis upon words. The title of each of its ten short chapters derives from some key statement within it, which takes on the force of a maxim or precept.

The characters of the story meet together in an informal circle. Out of school and unable, most of them, to find jobs because of the Depression, they turn to one another for companionship and consolation. Always in the background stands New York, Jacob Cohen's "capital of departure." With its "overwhelming presence," the city prohibits true community. The circle itself exists *faute de mieux*, and no one is willing to admit his dependence upon it. The members come together, as Jacob observes, "in order not to be alone, to escape from deviceless solitude."[26]

At the center of the group are Laura and Rudyard Bell, a brother and sister who live together. She, the only woman of the circle, is embittered because the Depression has spoiled her chances for marriage. Rudyard, toward whom she is by turns scornful and adoring, is a self-styled playwright, a deluded esthete utterly remote from the world and full of diffident self-love and false idealism. Like Samuel Hart in "The Child Is the Meaning of This Life," Rudyard spends a good deal of his time with children, with whom he attempts to pass as a sage. He has a certain childishness, which is shared by other members of the circle, who miss their schooldays and who play with ideas much as children play with toys.

The circle is like a family, and Laura is its mother, scolding and indulgent by turns. She is used by her friends, all of them men, and she knows it; but she is bound to her role by her own need to be needed. She is torn between love and repulsion, as her behavior toward Rudyard shows: "Laura's love and admiration of her brother did not prevent her from attempting to overthrow the attitudes in which Rudyard took the most pride. This was the way in which she tried to defend herself from the intensity of her love. . . ." Toward the others, she shows the same ambivalence: "Laura provided what each of them liked best, which did not prevent her from being ironic about their preferences and assuming the appearance of one who begrudges and denies all generous indulgence and attention."[27] Her irony is one instance of the irony that pervades the story as a whole.

Jacob's function is to be "the conscience or judge of the circle,"[28] and he necessarily stands somewhat apart from the others. He observes and analyzes his friends with a certain detachment, and he provides and comments at the end upon the maxim which is the story's title. At the same time, he is another character to the narrator; and as such, he too is exposed to irony. Seen as well as seeing, he is both object and subject, a mediating consciousness upon which the serious and comic strains of the story converge.

None of the other characters have the importance of these three. They are little more than voices that express various typical human attitudes and obsessions. Francis French, a promiscuous homosexual, illustrates in his own way the sterility of the circle as a whole. Edmund Kish, who suffers from pride of intellect, has an arrogance that keeps him from getting a job. Ferdinand Harrap is a figure of vanity, and Marcus Gross is exactly what his surname suggests. The names of the characters tend to be comic and pretentious in the manner of Shenandoah Fish. Some, like the name Israel Brown, a character hardly more than mentioned, are of Jewish provenance (here the comic effect is enhanced by the Anglo-Saxon surname); others may be gentile. With its intellectual passion, its search for moral meanings, and its satirical humor, the circle seems to be essentially Jewish in spirit.

As a study in irony, "The World Is a Wedding" continually resorts to Schwartz's "mock-grand style." One of its purposes is to satirize the intellectual earnestness and self-consciousness of the characters. The story opens in this key: "In this our life there are no beginnings but only departures.... Darkly rises each moment from the life which has been lived and which does not die, for each event lives in the heavy head forever, waiting to renew itself."[29] Jacob himself, as has been suggested, does not escape mild ridicule. Out for a walk, "Jacob, thinking about his friends...was borne forward by the feeling that through them he might know his own fate...." These friends "existed in his mind like great pictures in a famous gallery...."[30] The mockery not only qualifies Jacob's moral earnestness but also helps to lighten the pathos of his diminished life.

Elsewhere as well, pathos lies just beneath the seriocomic surface, as when Laura overhears her friends discussing a woman who has become engaged. "'What does she have that I don't have?'" she asks, conscious, of course, that the question is a stock one. She repeats it again and again during the evening. "Laura insisted in vain that her question be answered," says the narrator with "mock-grand" stiltedness; "and sometimes she placed her hands on her breasts lightly, as if in estimation, although when sober she was ashamed of any mention of sexual desire."[31]

The characters mock themselves and one another. A desperately playful spirit pervades their sententious observations, for they are aware that they are playing verbal games that will have no issue in action. They sometimes indulge in the narrator's own "mock-grand style," as when Jacob informs them, "'Love is the dark victor whom no one outwits,'"[32] which becomes the title of the sixth chapter.

"The World Is a Wedding" has one maxim above all, its title, which Jacob explains in the last chapter at a final party for the circle, now about to break up. Laura is bitter because she realizes that she has been used by her friends; and, distorting a short story by Kafka, she compares herself to a cow that is eaten alive by a hunter and his horse, who represent Rudyard and his friends.[33] Jacob tries to comfort her, telling her that "'we

all have each other and we all need each other,'"[34] and after
further altercation he delivers his precept: "'Does it mean anything? Yes, and it means everything. For example, it means that
the world is the wedding of God and Nature. This is the first
of all the marriages.'" He refers to "The Peasant Wedding," a
painting by Pieter Breughel: "'Do you remember what that
picture looks like? If you look at it long enough, you will see
all the parts that anyone and everyone can have.'"[35]

Jacob's speech is typical of his idealism. Laura objects sar-
castically, and Francis French describes the dreary wedding
of his own sister at the age of thirty-six. This wedding contrasts
to Breughel's painting, a rich and colorful picture of a group of
peasants at a marriage feast. But Jacob then describes the picture, which represents for him all the ages and conditions of
man at the wedding feast of life: "'And at this party there are
enough places and parts for everyone, and if no one can play
every part, yet everyone can come to ... the wedding feast. ...
He might as well be dead if he does not know that the world
is a wedding.'" The story ends with a sarcastic rebuttal by Laura:
"'You can't fool me, the world is a funeral. We are all going
to the grave, no matter what you say. Let me give all of you
one good piece of advice: *Let your conscience be your bride.*'"[36]

Jacob is calling for a loving approach to life that would trans-
form it and redeem it. His choice of a picture to illustrate his
precept suggests that this lovingness has its equivalent in the
vision of the artist, which has transformed the commonplace
scene of a village wedding. Francis' anecdote is a picture of life
without love—life untransformed and unredeemed. Laura's rebuttal arises from the extreme of "conscience," which signifies
consciousness, as in the poem "Far Rockaway," the analytic
reason that is at the opposite pole from the spirit of loving communion that Jacob enjoins. Jacob and Laura thus define the
familiar polarities of Schwartz's mind. As Politzer remarks,

Conscience ... is here only another name for consciousness, which
... is the antithesis and negation of life. This conscience, this consciousness, is the axis round which Schwartz's second, higher world
turns. Thus in the concluding dialogue ... the conflict between life
and intellect, between the unreflecting living-together and the con-
scientious recording and interpreting of every simple impulse, is

brought together. . . . And judging from his writings, there is little doubt that Schwartz would like to feel and think as Jacob does, but actually thinks and feels like Laura.[37]

Only in some of his last poems does Schwartz give a form to the point of view represented by Jacob, thereby abandoning the theme of the conflict between experience and consciousness; and in these poems artists are among the chief celebrants of his "summer knowledge," like Breughel in the present story.

CHAPTER 7

Vaudeville for a Princess and Other Poems

WHEN *Vaudeville for a Princess* appeared in 1950, the reviews were generally unfavorable. The fairest and most
balanced remarks were those of Rolfe Humphries, who wrote
in the *Nation* that "the poetry of Mr. Schwartz suffers its most
severe criticism at the hands of the author's own prose, for the
later is amusing, clever—if at times a bit glib—witty, bright,
full of satirical energy and bounce, in short, extremely readable,
whereas the verse tends to be solemn, owlish, abstract, tiresome,
and, to my ear at least, entirely earless."[1]

All in all, the items in this collection show a falling away
from the standards of Schwartz's earlier work. He knew this:
of the fifty-six poems in the collection, of which forty are sonnets,
he included in *Summer Knowledge* (or *Selected Poems*) only
"The Winter Twilight, Glowing Black and Gold"; "Starlight Like
Intuition Pierced the Twelve"; and "I Did Not Know the Spoils
of Joy." He might justifiably have chosen a few others as well.
Many of the poems appeared throughout the 1940's in *Accent,
Commentary,* the *Kenyon Review,* the *Nation,* the *Partisan Review,* and *Poetry.*

The first of its three parts, which gives the book its title, comprises a series of poems alternating with comic prose pieces that
somewhat resemble certain of the stories of *The World Is a
Wedding* in style, though with a broader humor. These include
burlesque interpretations of *Othello, Hamlet,* and the Don Juan
legend; personal anecdotes in which the poet mocks himself
and the literary world; a discussion of marriage and divorce;
and a comic definition of existentialism. The poems tend to be
more serious than the prose, but some of them try for a light-
heartedness. Schwartz notes beneath the title that it was "suggested by Princess [now Queen] Elizabeth's admiration of

Danny Kaye."[2] The whole book is a version of Schwartz's dream
theater, with the poet—who identifies himself with a Jewish
comedian—once again onstage as he was between the acts in
Coriolanus and His Mother. Queen Elizabeth, who is twice
referred to, humorously, in the text, resembles the famous persons
that appear in other works.

The second part of the collection, "The True, The Good and
the Beautiful," consists of eight poems whose central theme is
the greatness of poetry. Together they constitute an apologia
for being a poet in a world at war and in disorder. The third
and final part of the book, "The Early Morning Light," is a
sonnet sequence. The title, suggesting rebirth and beginning, is
played against the epigraph to the section, which is from "The
Crack-Up" by F. Scott Fitzgerald: "In the real dark night of the
soul, it is always three o'clock in the morning."[3]

In format, *Vaudeville for a Princess* tries to re-create the impression of a series of vaudeville acts by interspersing the sections and also the front matter with totally blank, black pages
that suggest theatrical blackouts. The book contains a number
of typographical oddities, for example, an imitation of Greek
script in the epigraph to the whole collection, a humorous
rendering of a passage in praise of love from Plato's *Symposium*.
Vaudeville for a Princess is dedicated to the poet's second wife,
Elizabeth Pollet, the princess's namesake.

I *Poetry*

In many of the poems of *Vaudeville for a Princess*, Schwartz
carries his obsession with poetry and the misfortunes of poets to
the farthest extreme, both in his theme and in his extensive—
and excessive—use of learned and literary epigraphs, allusions,
and the like. "There is an incestuous preoccupation with the
pathos of the existence of poets," noted the *Hudson Review*,
"which must be classed as self-pity; there is unguarded senti-
mentality and a haphazard and careless technique."[4] In some of
his lighter poems, it seems as if Schwartz were trying to dis-
arm criticism by insisting that he should not be taken too
seriously.

In any case, he rarely realizes in these poems the ideal of
nonchalant eloquence that he proposes in the opening poem
of the first part, "On a Sentence by Pascal:[5]

> "True eloquence mocks eloquence."
> Did that Frenchman mean
> That heroes are hilarious
> And orators obscene?
>
> Eloquence laughs at rhetoric,
> Is ill at ease in Zion,
> Or baa-baas like the lucid lamb,
> And snickers at the lion,
>
> And smiles, being meticulous,
> Because truth is ridiculous.

" 'My Mind to Me a Kingdom Is,' "[6] which follows, takes its title from the first line of a poem by Sir Edward Dyer (d. 1607). Schwartz's own first line, "The mind to me a North Pole is," suggests that he is about to parody the original, just as Lewis Carroll parodied Wordsworth and Southey in his Alice books. But Schwartz does not do so, although he continues to arouse the reader's expectations in the lines that follow:

> The mind to me a North Pole is,
> Superb the whiteness there I find,
> The glaring snows of consciousness
> Dazzle enough to make me blind. . . .

These lines are in contrast to Dyer's somewhat complacent rejoicing in a contained and controlled consciousness:

> My mind to me a kingdom is;
> Such perfect joy therein I find
> That it excels all other bliss
> Which God or nature hath assigned.[7]

Schwartz abandons this parallelism, referring to the first-person narrator of Henry James's *The Turn of the Screw*: "Until I see too much, in this/ Resembling James' governess." Only in that this governess is excessively conscious, and perhaps insane, does mention of her relate to the subject. Schwartz bases most of the rest of the poem upon references to events in the American Civil War, which is brought in by way of the first two lines of the second stanza: "The mind and self in Civil War/ Are locked and wasted, blocked and forced." Only in the last stanza does he again refer to the mind itself.

The next poem of this first section, "I Did Not Know the Spoils of Joy,"[8] beginning, "When that I was and a little tiny boy," incorporates lines from the song in *Twelfth Night.* Like the preceding poem, it has only a tangential relationship to its model, and little integrity and direction of its own. The poem appears in *Summer Knowledge* (or *Selected Poems*) with superfluous lines added to each of the last three stanzas. The next poem, "True Recognition Often Is Refused,"[9] starts off with an echo of Wordsworth, not the less powerful for being immediately curtailed. "We poets by the past and future used" recalls, if only with the first two words, the great lines from "Resolution and Independence": "We poets in our youth begin in gladness;/ But thereof come in the end despondency and madness."[10] Schwartz's poem is a rambling and abstract description of the sufferings of poets.

The next poem, "The Passionate Shepherd to His Love,"[11] alludes to Christopher Marlowe's poem by the same title and perhaps as well to John Donne's "The Bait." Schwartz soon departs from these originals (adding a couplet to their four-line stanza form) to ramble freely through a series of incoherent references: to Ghenghis Khan, Hallowe'en, and "Molière's bourgeois gentleman," among others. The inflated final stanza circles back to the point of departure:

> If these excursions seem to you
> Interesting as a rendezvous,
> > Rich as cake and revenue,
> > Handsome as hope and as untrue,
> > And full of travel's points of view,
> > Vivid as red and fresh as dew,
> Come live with me and try my life,
> And be my night, my warmth, my wife.

"The Masters of the Heart Touched the Unknown,"[12] besides its description of Baudelaire discussed in Chapter 3, comprises a number of other word portraits of the personalities and predicaments of some great writers and of one composer, Mozart. The poet celebrates their passion, their isolation, and their final glory as artists. Rehearsing "their passion's history," he finds solace in their example. Among others, he speaks of Keats, who "left for Italy to burn away"; of Hawthorne with his "endless guilt, his passion for the snow"; of Emily Dickinson who, "like heroines in Henry James," learned that "Renunciation like a tower remains/ Of Christ's great castle in the Western Heart./ And sang. And made a notebook of her art." The poem has passion of its own, but the two final stanzas are spoiled by the same inflated language that appears at the end of "The Passionate Shepherd to His Love" and by disconnected, incoherent imagery, an hysterical coda:

> They stood upon their heads. They thrust their hands
> In furnaces to find what they could bear.
> They climbed down pits and wells, and praised
> The wilderness, the future, and the truth.
> And in the end their separated heads
> Glared from a plate and criticized this life!

The next to the last poem of the section, "To Figaro in the Barbershop," has nothing to recommend it but its inoffensiveness. The concluding poem, however, "Starlight Like Intuition Pierced the Twelve,"[13] is undoubtedly the best in the book and one of Schwartz's finest achievements. The flatness, the unmusicality of its language, fulfills an artistic purpose, as it seldom does elsewhere in the collection, reflecting the disillusionment of the twelve disciples of Jesus, the speakers of the poem, with themselves and with the world after having witnessed the "unspeakable unnatural goodness" of their master. Their successive voices have a heavy tone that enforces the paradox of their desolation by the One who was supposed to bring about their salvation—the brilliant central idea of the poem:

> "I am as one native in summer places
> —Ten weeks' excitement paid for by the rich;
> Debauched by that and then all winter bored,"
> The sixth declared. "His peak left us a ditch!"
> "He came to make this life more difficult,"
> The seventh said, "No one will ever fit
> His measure's heights, all is inadequate:
> No matter what I do, what good is it?"

The language of the poem derives from ordinary speech, and it is frequently idiomatic, while metaphor is mostly simple, stark, and abstract. The paradoxical argument is embodied in the most commonplace images, such as "His peak left us a ditch!" or, toward the end, "too much goodness is a boomerang." At the same time, the poem has a certain rhetorical stateliness, as the stanza just quoted shows; and exclamations resembling those of traditional poetry find a foil in conversational locutions, as in the fourth stanza: "Vision, imagination, hope or dream,/ Believed, denied, the scene we wished to see?/ It does not matter in the least. . . ." The poem successfully fuses the poet's modern voice with a traditional tone, just as it gives a modern and distinctively personal interpretation to a religious subject.

The eight poems that comprise the second part of the collection, "The True, the Good and the Beautiful," while tending to be garrulous and slack, are partly successful. "Lunas Are Tempting to Old Consciousness," the fifth of the series, is addressed to "Dear Citizens," the world at large to which the poet wants to justify himself. Its setting, an amusement park by the seashore, recalls "Far Rockaway" and "In Dreams Begin Responsibilities." Like the earlier poem, it describes the public's desire to escape from consciousness—thrill seekers take dangerous rides as a relief from the burden of being alive. Perhaps, the poet suggests, they are courting final oblivion, death:

> Hark, from the coiling track come screams like jazz,
> As if they jumped from brinks of a burning house.
> How much some love the gross and plunging shock
> As if the screeching broke the block to luck!
> > Why do they hate their lives
> > Why do they wish to die?
> > Believing in vicious lies,
> > Afraid to remember and cry.
> Nearby in little caves a little train
> Seeks mystery and darkness like a vine.
> Upon a wheel the couples are revolved,
> As if tomorrow's blank had been resolved.[14]

The poem that follows, "Disorder Overtakes Us All Day Long,"[15] contrasts the lies and the trivia that form "the fresh news of the age" with the poet's commitment to the true, the good, and the beautiful. " 'Elizabeth would like to be a horse!' " reads one headline, to which he rejoins, "(Though she'll be Queen of England, in due course.)" He concludes:

Awed or indifferent, bemused or ill at ease
We who are poets play the game which is
A deadly earnest searching of all hearts
As if we struggled with a puzzle's parts,

Making the huge assumption that there is
A lucid picture which these fragments fit,
Disheveled in our clumsy, pious hands,
A picture true, good, and appropriate,

Raised up, like Joseph, from the unjust pit.
—And suppose that we are wrong? and in all pathos
We handled foolishly essential chaos?
                                        What then?
What but with patient hope to try again?

The last poem of the series, "The Past's Great Power Over-powers Every Hour,"[16] touches upon Schwartz's typical atti-tude toward the "obscene play," the past: "We live upon the past and day by day/ The past destroys us." He also presents the familiar idea that the self is the supreme object of one's search, and that it is inescapable: "... everywhere you tour, you take yourself." The last lines of the poem appropriately end the series itself: "Awake, my dears, and be deceived no more:/ What is our hope, except to tell the truth?"

The sonnets that make up the third part of the collection, "The Early Morning Light," are almost without exception ram-bling and incoherent in their development, and the rhyme scheme is handled arbitrarily. Humphries says, "... it's no good to rhyme *capital* and *beautiful,* or *stockings* and *markings,*—and it's no good to tell me these are calculated ironic effects, either."[17]

There is little real emotion in these sonnets. They are full of rhetorical shouts, such as "Poor Poe! and cursèd poets every-where," which begins the sestet of the lugubriously entitled "'My Love, My Love, My Love, Why Have You Left Me Alone?'"[18] "She Lives with the Furies of Hope and Despair"[19] starts with an invocation: "O Jan Vermeer of Delft, descend, come near/ The Hudson and the West's last capital." The poem as a whole exemplifies Schwartz's desperate habit of throwing allusions together in the hope of producing a poetic effect. The woman referred to in the title is compared to Ophelia; "the daughter of the Swan," or Helen; and "statues of the classic age." Conceivably, these references might cohere in another poem, but in the present context they seem arbitrary.

II Prose

The prose of *Vaudeville for a Princess* is by and large better than the poetry. These short pieces have gaiety and humor, and sometimes a serious intent underlies the bright surface, like the look of somber eyes beneath the painted mask of a clown. The first sketch, "Existentialism: The Inside Story," proposes that taking a bath is a primary existential situation: *"Existentialism means that no one else can take a bath for you."* This example derives from Heidegger, "who points out that no one else can die for you. You must die your own death."[20] As bathing is a daily act, it can be thought of without revulsion, unlike death. Also, taking a bath "involves the vital existentialist emphasis on choice: you can choose *not* to take a bath, you can waver in your choice, you can finally decide to take a bath, the whole drama of human freedom can become quite hectic or for that matter quite boring." Taking a bath is "an *extreme situation*," for "God knows what may occur to you when you are in the tub, you may decide to drown yourself because existence, as existentialists say, is essentially *absurd....*"[21] The sketch concludes with a comic definition of the basis of existentialism: *"Human beings exist."* Therefore, "if you really exist as a human being, you have no need of any explanation of existence or existentialism."[22]

In "The Ego Is Always at the Wheel" Schwartz comments upon the American passion for owning automobiles and upon the Depression, among other things; and he exposes himself to mild ridicule for brooding over missed chances and for pursuing success. The piece is chiefly interesting for its revelation of character. Mocking both America and himself, he confesses that he is "passionate with reveries of glory and power, of riding up Fifth Avenue under great snowstorms of ticker-tape, in a beautiful open limousine, cheered by admiring throngs."[23] Another sketch with autobiographical implications is "Fun with the Famous, Stunned by the Stars," which describes the idiosyncrasies of certain unnamed famous poets and the rivalry existing in literary circles. It is preceded by a sinister epigraph: "*Fame corrupts, absolute fame corrupts absolutely, all great men are insane.*"[24]

"The Difficulty of Divorce" ridicules laws that make adultery the only grounds for divorce. Schwartz relates the story of a woman acquaintance who became her own correspondent in her divorce case in order to avoid difficulties. He also objects to the expurgation of a passage from the marriage formula in *The Book of Common Prayer*, according to which the bride promised to be "bonour and buxom" in bed and at board. Schwartz modernizes the expression to "buxom and *débonair.*" The old ceremony, he believes, was more candid because it accepted the sexual side of marriage. The deletion of the phrase "illustrates how people have not been paying the proper attention to marriage, and how the institution as a whole is in a parlous state...." He invites Princess Elizabeth, who "will be the secular head of the Church of England ... to do something about the whole affair in this very important matter of what is said at the very start of the marriage by the bride to the groom...."[25]

In his three sketches on literary subjects—*Hamlet, Othello,* and Don Juan, or Don Giovanni, after the Mozart opera—Schwartz retells the stories in modern American English and searches for motivations. In "Hamlet, or There Is Something Wrong with Everyone," he says of the Freudian explanation of Hamlet's anger at his mother's remarriage: "According to this view of his conduct, he was jealous of his uncle and in love with his mother, who was still a very attractive woman."[26] As in his stories, Schwartz uses idiomatic or conventional phrases that add a touch of absurdity to his deadpan discussion of serious subjects or theories of his own innovation, as is the case in the following: "People have been arguing for hundreds of years about what was really wrong with Hamlet. Some say that he must have been a woman, some say that he was a homosexual ... and there is one fascinating view which maintains that all the mystery is utterly clarified if we suppose that everyone is roaring drunk from the beginning to the end of the play." He concludes with another far-fetched interpretation, seemingly facetious but in fact self-confessional, proposing, "for what it is worth, and to use clinical terms," that Hamlet was manic-depressive. "No one knows what the real causes of the manic-depressive disorder are, whether physical or mental or both, and that is why no one understands Hamlet."[27]

His discussion of *Othello*, "Iago, or the Lowdown on Life," resembles his approach to *Hamlet*. The villain's inscrutable malignity becomes the point of critical surmise. He declares that "Iago had no good reason for hating Othello the way he did," a restatement in plain English of "the motive-hunting of a motiveless malignity" proposed by Coleridge, "an expert on German philosophy, indecision, and laudanum." Shakespeare himself is not spared: "He must have been a very unhappy man, even though very talented. He seems to be saying that all he can say is that Desdemona is in her grave."[28]

In "Don Giovanni, or Promiscuity Resembles Grapes," Schwartz again resorts to Freudian theory. Did the hero sleep with and then abandon so many women because none of them resembled his mother, or because they all resembled his mother ("incest is wrong"), or because he was revenging himself upon his father? "All of these theories may or may not be true," Schwartz concludes; "but after one has reviewed all of them and weighed them critically, there is only one conclusion one can feel any certainty about, namely, that Giovanni was a Lesbian, that is to say, someone who likes to sleep with girls."[29]

CHAPTER *8*

"The Kingdom of Heaven on Earth
on Sunday Summer Day"

SCHWARTZ'S later poems form the second part of *Summer Knowledge* (1959) and appear in it under that title, which also became the subtitle of *Selected Poems,* the New Directions paperback reprint. Some of them were first published in magazines, notably the *Kenyon Review,* the *New Republic,* the *New Yorker,* the *Partisan Review,* and *Poetry.* Included among them are three poems from *Vaudeville for a Princess* and "Lincoln," an excerpt from *Genesis.*

Most of the new poems differ in both form and theme from Schwartz's earlier work. They show an attempt to break away from the conventions of formal verse, to which he had adhered with sometimes brilliant effect in the beginning but had mishandled for the most part in *Vaudeville for a Princess.* Most of the new poems also try to impart a vision of a kind of knowledge —the "summer knowledge" of the title—which is intuitive rather than analytical and which is, above all, exemplified by the works of artists, poets, and musicians, whom Schwartz now celebrates not as "culture heroes" enduring the martyrdom of isolation, but rather as celebrants and seers endowed with a transcendent and life-transforming vision. These poems represent a heroic, if only partly successful, effort to break away from the poet's past preoccupations—from an obsession with exile and the ironies of introspective and retrospective knowledge. With this change, there is one of scene: the poet leaves the city and turns to the natural world for his images.

Free verse predominates, and some of the poems are reminiscent of Walt Whitman. "Seurat's Sunday Afternoon along the Seine," for example, suggests Whitman's use of accumulated pictorial detail and his syntactical repetitions:

115

A young man blows his flute, curved by pleasure's
          musical activity,
His back turned upon the Seine, the sunlight, and
          the sunflower day.
A dapper dandy in a top hat gazes idly at the Seine:
The casual delicacy with which he holds his cane
Resembles his tailored elegance.
He sits with well-bred posture, sleek and pressed,
Fixed in his niche: he is his own mustache.
A working man slouches parallel to him, quite comfortable,
Lounging or lolling, leaning on his elbow, smoking a
          meerschaum. . . .[1]

The tone of the new poems is often invocative, in keeping
with the poet's new role as celebrant and seer. Here too one
finds an echo of Whitman, as in this passage from "Vivaldi":

O clear soprano like the morning peal of the bluebells,
O the watercolors of the early morning,
con amore and *vivace!* dancing, prancing, galloping, rollicking![2]

To produce an incantatory effect, Schwartz relies heavily,
often excessively, upon internal rhyme and alliteration. In the
last line of "A Little Morning Music," he describes light as
"Gazing and blazing, blessing and possessing all vividness and
all darkness."[3] In "Gold Morning, Sweet Prince" he says that
"our little life . . . is what it is/ Because of love accepted, re-
jected, refused and jilted, faded, raided, neglected or betrayed."[4]
Similar lines appear in many of the new poems.

I   "The First Morning of the Second World"

The best way to define "summer knowledge" may be to look
at the poems which themselves attempt a definition. One of
these, "The First Morning of the Second World," is, as its title
suggests, about birth, or genesis, so often symbolized by morning. More precisely, this birth into "the second world" is a
rebirth following a death—that of the old self obsessed with
itself—into the world of "summer knowledge." The poem is
far from being one of Schwartz's best, for it is verbose and
confusingly abstract; but it is interesting as a record of the
conversion of two of the primary images of his earlier poems,
the blue sky and the snow.

A visionary poem of transformation, "The First Morning of the Second World" opens with a forbidding winter scene. The poet describes himself as a hunter of birds in a "pathless wood" that recalls the opening lines of *The Divine Comedy*. The metaphor pictures the mind in the act of stalking itself. The poet is "locked/ And intent in that vigil in which the hunter is hunted/ As the mind is, seeking itself, falconer, falcon and hawk, victor and victim,/ Aware of the dry river beds, the droughts of the little deaths...." Yet in the very depths of his privation he finds grace. As "the gun of the mind" takes aim, he hears:

> ... the rush not of the birds rising from bush and thicket
> thrashing and clacking,
> But suddenly the pouring continuous sibilance of waterfalls,
> Certainly and suddenly, for a moment's eternity, it was the
> Ecstasy and stillness of the white
> Wizard blizzard, the white god fallen, united,
> Entirely whiteness
> The color of forgiveness, beginning and hope.[5]

This whiteness becomes the very light of the ensuing vision, in which it is "also all the colors flaring, melting, or flowing."[6] *Genesis*, as it has been noted, anticipates this change of snow, "the death of the colored world," into light, "the heroine of every picture." The transformation offers a clue to the nature of "summer knowledge." Light, the actual medium of vision, is not only a glory in itself, but it also symbolizes the spiritual vision of the seer. In the light of this knowledge, the poet "sees" that the world is divine; and he perceives at one and the same time the unity and diversity of the world.

Just as the snow is transformed into light, so the blue sky—now no longer "inexorable" as in "Socrates' Ghost Must Haunt Me Now," or the inscrutable "eye of God" in which the tormented Dr. Bergen believes—is brought to earth as a reflection upon the river that is the setting of this poem, "the river of summer, blue as the infinite curving blueness above...."[7] The river is covered with little boats that contain the poet's friends. His eyes open upon a vision of the past, a blessed retrospect: "There hope was, and the hopes, and the years past,/ The beings I had known and forgotten and half-remembered or remembered too often...." He sees the past now not as he saw it earlier, as a comic and pathetic photograph, diminished in the distance of time, but as an eternal moment in which everyone and everything has been gloriously transfigured. In this vision, he enters into communion with his lost friends: "They were with me, and they were me, I was them, forever united/ As we all moved forward in a consonance silent and moving/ Seated and gazing,/ Upon the beautiful river forever."[8]

He describes himself and his friends as "children on the painted wooden horses, rising and falling, of the carnival's carousel. . . ." The carousel, or merry-go-round, appears in *Genesis* and "In Dreams Begin Responsibilities" as a symbol of mindless, mechanical motion in time, like the wheeling earth, the rolling ball, and other such images. Here, however, it symbolizes wholeness and completeness, a blissful and dancelike harmony. The carousel turns to "a small music" that seems to be saying, " 'The task is round, the round is the task, the task and the round are a dance, and/ There is nothing to think but drink of love and knowledge. . . .' "[9]

This love, linked with "knowledge," is compared to light, which "alone gives all colors being," and as such represents at one and the same time both "unity and distinction." In the act of love, the moment of knowledge and the moment of experience, hopelessly far apart in Schwartz's earlier work, coincide. Love is "the gratification of action by those who enact it and at once/ In the enacting behold it. . . ." The rift between subject and object, knower and known, is finally closed. In love, "The self is another but with and wholly the self, loving and beloved/ . . . passing from both beyond to the being of being/ Self-hooded selfhood seeks in the darkness and daylight blind and lost."[10]

When the poet apprehends this truth, he undergoes a rebirth, a "waking in the first morning to a world outside of whiteness united,/ Transfigured, possessed by the blessedness of whiteness and light. . . ." This whiteness is light and "more than light"; it is "the inner morning and meaning of all light." The moment of waking is like the moment "when Adam first looked upon another self, a self like his own self, yet an absolute other and newness. . . ." It is like "the little moment" when the reborn Lazarus was summoned from his grave by "Jesus, snow and morning."[11]

II "The Fulfillment"

There is pathos as well as joy in "The First Morning of the Second World," for, though the poet comes to understand the nature of love, he is "too late," to echo a ghost in *Genesis*. The past tense dominates the poem: life and its possibilities, its hopes, are looked back upon. One finds the same pathos in "The Fulfillment,"[12] in which the poet seems to be contemplating the past from beyond the grave. Like "The First Morning," which it precedes and introduces, this poem presents a vision of unity, a merging that yet does not abolish individuality. Here also the river and the carousel are symbols of harmony:

> Where we were, if we were there, serene and shining
> Each being sang and moved with the sleekness of rivers,
> United in a choir, many and one, as the spires of
>   flames in fire,
> Flowing and perfected, flourishing and fulfilled forever,
> Rising and falling as the carousel. . . .

However, this vision is of the unreclaimable past; and consciousness, as in *Genesis*, is accompanied by a sense of damnation. A companion, the "fellow" of the first line, who is perhaps another voice of the narrator, his questioned self replying, says, " 'We are condemned because this is our consciousness.' "

Only from the vantage point of death, that of the ghosts in *Genesis*, can the narrator and his "fellow" see that the life that has been lost contained possibilities of love and order which they were unaware of at the time:

> Then, when at last we knew where we had come,
> It was then that we saw what was lost as we knew
>   where we had been
> (Or knew where we had been as we saw all that
>   was lost!)
> And knew for the first time the richness and poverty
> Of what we had been before and were no more,
> The striving, the suffering, the dear dark hooded
>   mortality
> Which we had been and never known. . . .

III "Summer Knowledge"

These poems, though they describe states of harmonious being and knowing, are reminiscent of earlier attitudes and points of view. But in the title poem, "Summer Knowledge,"[13] which immediately follows "The First Morning of the Second World," Schwartz breaks completely with his past work and turns to the natural world for images. The movement of nature describes an organic cycle through the seasons, from the birth that is spring to the death that is winter, and then begins anew. So, "summer knowledge" is of the whole, not merely of an aspect of the whole:

> Summer knowledge is not the winter's truth, the
> truth of fall, the autumn's fruition. . . .
> It is not May knowledge, little and leafing and
> growing green. . . .

Rather, "Summer knowledge is . . . the knowledge of growing and the supple recognition of the fullness and the fatness and the roundness of ripeness." It is knowledge as symbolized by the fruit, whose roundness is an image of the seasonal cycle of which it is the fulfillment. The moment of fullness is also the moment of death, but out of death new life will begin. "Summer knowledge" is "phoenix knowledge"; it is "the knowledge of death as birth,/ Of death as the soil of all abounding flowering flaring rebirth." Intuitive rather than intellectual, such knowledge is described variously throughout the poem as "bird knowledge," "cat knowledge," and "deer knowledge," as opposed to "the knowledge of lore and learning."

The poem is a detailed catalogue of instances as to what "summer knowledge" is and what it is not, but the result is less than a poem. One is left with the feeling that Schwartz has written about a poem he would have liked to write. Innumerable details, abstract descriptions of exalted states of being, an ardent tone of voice, have not produced poetry; and the use of rhyme and alliteration fails to conceal an underlying prosaic flatness. This statement is true not only of "Summer Knowledge" but also of "The First Morning" and "The Fulfillment," despite outstanding lines, and of all too many other later poems, interesting though it may be to trace their development from earlier themes and images. There is sometimes a hysterical striving for effect, and often the emotion that the poet undoubtedly feels fails to get into form.

Still, despite these grave reservations, there is enough real poetry in Schwartz's later work, either as individual poems or as parts of poems, to indicate that he might have made a more forceful and beautiful statement of his new insights had his psychic health and the conditions of his life been better.

IV "Seurat's Sunday Afternoon along the Seine"

Among Schwartz's more successful later poems is "Seurat's Sunday Afternoon along the Seine," his most descriptive and definite statement of his new approach to art and reality. Though the poem is sometimes long-winded and abstract, it is one in which one senses a steady growth of the poet's vision. Vision—as that implies both the physical sense of sight and the deeper, intuitive vision of the imagination—is a term that is particularly applicable to this poem and to the painting of which it is the verbal re-creation. Properly known in French as "Un Dimanche à la Grande-Jatte," and in English as "Sunday Afternoon on the Grand Jatte" (1884–86), this painting is the most important work of Georges Seurat and one of the main achievements of Postimpressionism.

Seurat employed the technique known as pointillism, whereby a painter built up color on the canvas by juxtaposing points or dots of pure color, which are optically combined by the viewer. For example, blue dots and yellow dots next to one another produce at a distance the effect of green, while complementary colors in juxtaposition, such as red with green, yellow with violet, orange with blue, harmonize with and intensify each other. The technique has a basis in optical science: the infinitely various colors that the eye perceives result from optical combinations of prismatic colors, into which light, itself colorless or white, is broken. The purpose of pointillism was to produce a luminous effect that would be esthetically equivalent to the effect of light itself.

Mosaiclike dots of color are the basic units of Seurat's paintings; but, on the other hand, he was much concerned with the formal aspects of his art. According to the poem, "he is at once poet and architect,/ Seeking complete evocation in forms as strong as the Eiffel Tower...." He makes "a mosaic of the little dots into a mural of the splendor of order...."[14] In both the arrangement of color and the construction of his paintings, Seurat was a theorist who carefully deliberated his effects. While Impressionistic, his work has a classical balance and serenity; and his scenes are both momentary and timeless.

Schwartz was attracted to Seurat and in particular to his "Dimanche à la Grande-Jatte" because the painter's technique objectifies the poet's own conception of light as "the heroine of every picture," as he says in *Genesis*, and as "white, a milk whiteness, and also all the colors flaring, melting, or flowing," according to "The First Morning of the Second World." Also, the painter's concern with theory appealed to Schwartz's intellect. Meyer Schapiro believes that the poet "responded to the intellectual power of Seurat in the strict conception and application of a new method. Seurat as a painter unites the scientific and the poetic-meditative as no other modern artist has done...."[15]

In an article on the painter, Schapiro says that Seurat is at once "the exact mind, fanatic about its methods and theories, and the poetic visionary absorbed in contemplating the mysterious light and shadow of a transfigured domain." He is "the visionary of the seen." Influenced by the classical paintings of Pierre Puvis de Chavannes, Seurat "transformed the Golden Age ... into a golden day, the familiar idyll of Parisians on the sunny banks of the Seine." He portrays "a society that enjoys the world in a pure contemplation and calm."[16] The moment thus seen in Seurat's picture is an eternal present, or in Schwartz's own words in his poem, "The kingdom of heaven on earth on Sunday summer day."[17]

Not only in technique but also in subject—a crowd partaking of a Sunday communion, partaking of the sacramental light—the painting is a visualization of Schwartz's own conception of "summer knowledge." In its setting and in its subject, the poem about Seurat's picture resembles "The First Morning of the Second World," but it is better realized, no doubt because the poet found in the painting an objective form whose images helped to fix his own ideas and emotions.

The painting portrays a crowd of people taking their leisure on a grassy bank of the Seine in the calm fullness of a summer afternoon, bathed in a light that is at once momentary and eternal, arrested in attitudes of monumental repose. The people "are looking at hope itself, under the sun, free from the teething anxiety, the gnawing nervousness/ Which wastes so many days and years of consciousness." The light that fills the picture seems to emanate from the painter himself, who is effaced, "unseen." Seurat is "dedicated radiance, supreme concentration, fanatically threading/ The beads, needles and eyes ... of vividness and permanence."[18] Later he is described as wanting "to hold the warm leisure and pleasure of the holiday/ Within the fiery blaze and passionate patience of his gaze and mind/ Now and forever...."[19]

The poet, as the beholder of the painting, participates in the vision of the artist, re-creating it with words; and the people within the painting are themselves looking. The fact of their looking endows them with their curious, characteristic stillness, the stillness of absolute waiting, waiting that is an end in itself. Looking is a form of communion with the light: "Many are looking, many are holding something or someone/ Little or big...." Some hold parasols, or umbrellas, whose curves the arching trees and the arching day itself repeat. Caught in this plenitude of light, one woman seems to have "turned to stone, or become a boulder," while "a little girl holds to her mother's arm/ As if it were a permanent genuine certainty...."

The description of the crowd culminates in a portrayal of a bourgeois married couple who "are each other's property," who seem to be "unaware or free of time, and the grave,/ Master and mistress of Sunday's promenade—of everything!" The artist with his transforming vision teaches that

> If you look long enough at anything
> It will become extremely interesting;
> If you look very long at anything
> It will become rich, manifold, fascinating:
>
> If you can look at any thing for long enough,
> You will rejoice in the miracle of love....[20]

The artist's vision is not limited to an exalted or special subject. Like other innovators of his time, he turns to the daily life of Paris for his motifs. Here he paints an everyday gathering from which no one is excluded: "The Sunday summer sun shines equally and voluptuously/ Upon the rich and the free, the comfortable, the *rentier,* the poor, and those who are paralyzed by poverty." He gives a classic poise to the commonplaces of the moment: "O happy, happy throng,/ It is forever Sunday, summer, free: you are forever warm...."[21] There is an echo in these lines of Keats's "Ode on a Grecian Urn," one of the greatest of the poems that celebrate works of art; but Seurat is far from Keats's "Tempe or the dales of Arcady," far from the classic "cold pastoral" sanctified by tradition. The Golden Age, as Schapiro has noted, has been brought into the present.

After further praise, in which Seurat is compared to great creators such as Mozart, Flaubert, and John Augustus Roebling, the builder of Brooklyn Bridge, and after further description of the painting itself, Schwartz returns to the idea that the commonplace, which the artist exalts and transforms, is holy:

> This is the celebration of contemplation,
> This is the conversion of experience to pure attention,
> Here is the holiness of all the little things
> Offered to us, discovered for us, transformed into the
>   vividest consciousness,
> After the shallowness or blindness of experience...."

The painter redeems one's vision from "the blurring, dirtying sooted surfaces which, since Eden and since birth,/ Make all the little things trivial or unseen...."[22] He restores one to the purity of genesis. He presents one, Schwartz says toward the end of the poem, with "Icons of purified consciousness."[23] Like Breughel, whose "Peasant Wedding" illustrates "The World Is a Wedding," Seurat offers a vision of the everyday world transformed by art.

Yet, even in "Seurat's Sunday Afternoon along the Seine" the poet depicts estrangement. The poem ends:

> Can we not also hear
> The voice of Kafka, forever sad, in despair's
>   sickness trying to say:
> "Flaubert was right: *Ils sont dans le vrai!*
> ....

They all stretch out their hands to me: but
they are too far away!"[24]

Briefly but significantly Schwartz once again describes the
familiar relationship between a scene of life and a removed
observer. Within the frame, the figures of the painting live on in
their eternal afternoon. Outside, the estranged poet—Kafka represents him—looks upon a world of happiness and fulfillment
from which he is barred.

V "Gold Morning, Sweet Prince"

"Seurat's Sunday Afternoon along the Seine" appropriately
concludes a section entitled "The Kingdom of Poetry," a group
of poems that celebrate art and artists. "Gold Morning Sweet
Prince," which opens the section, is worthy of note as a poem
in praise of Shakespeare that is both whimsical and devout,
in the spirit of the punning title. Shakespeare is "prince of
Avon"; he has transcended his family name, becoming royal in
his universality. His wisdom is "as immense/ As the sea is." He
shows life in all of its dimensions. Like God Himself, "he saw
what was and what is and what has yet to come to be. . . ."[25]
He teaches one that love is the motive of life—love betrayed as
well as love fulfilled, love that embraces opposites, that is "kind
and cruel,/ Generous and unjust, heartless and irresistible, pain-
ful to the savant and gentle to the fool. . . ." The only alternative to loving is "Never to love, seeking immunity, discovering
nothingness."[26] The fullness of Shakespeare's vision can only
bring delight, even when he portrays tragic figures, because the
vision is of love, to be chosen at all costs over "nothingness." The
final lines celebrate the redeeming power of love and of Shakespeare himself; and the morning and the morning light signify
as always beginning and hope:

> Gold morning, sweet prince, black night has always
>   descended and has always ended,
> Gold morning, prince of Avon, sovereign and king
> Of reality, hope, and speech, may all the angels sing
> With all the sweetness and all the truth with which
>   you sang of anything and everything.[27]

VI *Three Letters*

"Sterne," "Swift," and "Baudelaire" are monologues in which Schwartz assumes the identities of these writers and imitates their epistolary styles. As in the poem on Seurat, he escapes from subjective vagueness in each instance by means of a given form—an imaginary letter. Laurence Sterne's is to Eliza Draper, a young married woman whom Sterne met in London and for whom he formed a sentimental attachment. His letters, which he wrote in the form of a journal and never sent, were intended to solace himself while he awaited her return from India, where she had sailed to join her husband, an official in the East India service. Sterne knew at the time that he was dying and that he would probably never see her again—which did, in fact, prove to be the case. Jonathan Swift writes to his Stella, or Hester Johnson, and her friend Rebecca Dingley. The imaginary letter of Charles Baudelaire typifies the poet's unhappy correspondence with his mother, in which he continually complained about debts and the indignity of having been assigned a guardian.

These poems stand somewhat apart from the others in the section in that they resemble Schwartz's earlier portrayals of the artist as an exile, a lonely sufferer; but his assumption here of other voices is an innovation, for in his earlier work the fictional "I" or persona was usually a direct extension of himself. All three letters are addressed to absent, beloved women, and all are laments by writers whose lives, like Schwartz's own, were full of despondency and a sense of ineluctable loneliness. Sterne tells Eliza, ". . . Love, alas, has fled with thee/ Whom all the night my wakeful eyes/ (While all the day is blind to me!)/ Imagine, summon, idolize. . . ."[28] The essence of Swift's personality is in his brief portrait of himself as one who is "astonished by the gush of vanity/ The stone and eyes of pride—yet equally/ By the least straw or glitter of nobility!"[29] And Baudelaire's accusation sums up his hopeless sense of injustice and his bondage to the past: "You are always armed to stone me, always:/ It is true. It dates from childhood."[30]

Though the poems are imaginary epitomes, they resemble actual letters in a number of instances. The opening line of the above passage from "Sterne" derives from a remark in his letter of April 29, 1767: "Love alas! was [*sic*] fled with thee

Eliza!"[31] The most striking adaptation are the lines, "—How soothable the heart is, dear Eliza!/ Supported when it sinks pathetically/ By a poor beast purring harmoniously!"[32] This paraphrases a passage in Sterne's letter of July 8, 1767: "—how soothable my heart is Eliza, when such little things sooth it! for in some pathetic sinkings I feel even some support from this poor Cat—I attend to her purrings—& think they harmonize me—"[33] Similarly, the last stanza of "Swift" paraphrases a passage from his letter of March 21, 1713.

VII   "The Kingdom of Poetry" *and Other Poems*

"Hölderlin," which is grouped with the three letters, is a weak, emotional effusion that does not merit its place; and the title poem of the section is another failure. Schwartz again indulges in the fallacy of imagining that poetry can be made by accumulating abstract and descriptive terms such as "hope," "success," "victory," "blessedness," "reality," "magnificent," and the like. The words denote conditions and qualities that may be sublime, beautiful, and otherwise desirable; but poetry cannot be evoked by abstract description alone. It is useless, for example, to say that poetry "magnifies and heightens reality," or that "reality is various and rich," or that "without poetry, reality is speechless or incoherent...."[34] Whatever value such statements may have as saying the truth about poetry, they are not in themselves poetic. Nor are they acceptable as prose— it is unlikely that Schwartz would have permitted himself to make such pronouncements in the course of a critical article. The verse form here is merely a means of self-indulgence, literary escapism; it condones a suspension of both the poetic and critical faculties.

Schwartz is better when he uses metaphor:

> For poetry is gay and exact. It says:
> "The sunset resembles a bull-fight.
> A sleeping arm feels like soda, fizzing."[35]

Ironically, "The Kingdom of Poetry" is neither "gay" nor "exact." It betrays its own definition. For the rest, it is noteworthy that Schwartz defines poetry with the thematic images of light and

the blue sky: "For poetry is like light, and it is light./ It shines
over all, like the blue sky, with the same blue justice."[36]

"Vivaldi," which follows the opening poem on Shakespeare, also
indulges in abstract terms and declamatory affirmations; but this
poem is redeemed here and there by vivid metaphors, such as:

> Remorse, here is the scar of healing,
> Here is a window, curiosity!
> And here, O sensuality, a sofa![37]

However, such playful flashes are buried in the surrounding
verbiage.

Other later poems worthy of note are, " 'I Am Cherry Alive,'
the Little Girl Sang," from the section "Morning Bells," in
which Schwartz again avoids formless subjectivity, by assuming
the voice of a child who is rejoicing in her world and in her
powers of self-transformation: " 'I am red, I am gold, I am
green, I am blue,/ I will always be me, I will always be new!' "[38]
In the same section, "The True-Blue American" and "The
Would-Be Hungarian," which respectively dramatize American
attitudes and the search for American identity, are verbose
and stridently euphoric; but they are redeemed in part by the
poet's psychological insight and by his skillful presentation of
anecdotal detail. The other poems of the section, as the title
itself announces, celebrate the advent of the morning light and
the beauty and innocence of the natural world.

The last two sections of the book, "The Deceptive Present,
The Phoenix Year" and "The Phoenix Choir," contain some of
the least successful of the later poems, although lines that belong
in a worthier context can be found among them. Most of the
poems are marred by the garrulity and abstractness that have
been noted so often, and they do not elaborate in any significant
way the themes that have already been discussed.[39] As always,
Schwartz comes closest to success when he avails himself of
some means of objectivity, whether by following a more or
less formal pattern, as in "The Foggy, Foggy Blue," a poem that
wryly celebrates the beauties of deception after a lifetime of
seeking the unmasked truth, or by keeping to specific, concrete
observations and memories, as in "During December's Death":
"The dusk was black although, elsewhere, the first star in the

cold sky suddenly whistled,/ And I thought I heard the fresh scraping of the flying steel of boys on roller skates/ Rollicking over the asphalt in 1926. . . ."[40] This is poetry; this is beautiful.

VIII *Conclusion*

Schwartz's later poems, while differing from his earlier work, are related to it in theme in that they depict an alternative and complementary way of interpreting the world—another form of "knowledge." To describe such knowledge, he uses certain central images that appear earlier, but that later assume a different value or undergo a transformation, the most remarkable of which is the change of snow into light, anticipated in *Genesis*. Turning from his preoccupation with the past, he celebrates the present world and the present moment, the only eternity. Knowledge is immediate and intuitive rather than retrospective and analytic. The self communes and merges with the world while yet retaining its distinction, its identity. This "summer knowledge" is compared to love, and its predominant symbol is light.

In Schwartz's earlier work the very condition for knowing the world is separation, in time, above all. There, the reality of the self and the reality of others can never be reconciled, and transcendence is represented largely by the sky's "inexorable blue" or by the unearthly whiteness of the snow. Though it may have a hopeful aspect, the snow also suggests the oblivion of sleep and death, which alone can heal the wounds of consciousness. The later work is largely an attempt to dramatize a more congenial form of "knowledge," whereby rifts are closed, the sky descends to earth, and the whiteness of the snow becomes the whiteness of light, the source of all color, all distinction, which it preserves and enfolds.

This thematic and symbolic synthesis gives a coherent pattern to a body of work that varies greatly in quality. Yet, while it is interesting to trace its development, it cannot confer value upon the work. Rather, it ultimately receives whatever value it may have from the work. It is always difficult to judge a writer as recently dead as Schwartz and to estimate him in relation to his contemporaries. It seems safe to say, however, while allowing for the slight possibility that unpublished work may prove the contrary to be true, that Schwartz will not have a place among the preeminent poets and writers of his generation; for although his best writing is at a very high level, he did not reach this level often enough.

Indiscriminate publishing has tended to obscure his real excellence. An ideal collection of his creative work, according to the assessment of this survey, would include a number of his early poems in his first collection; the stories in *The World Is a Wedding*, above all, "In Dreams Begin Responsibilities"; a handful of poems from *Vaudeville for a Princess*, including "Starlight Like Intuition Pierced the Twelve"; a few prose pieces from the same work; the poems recommended in this chapter, in particular those on Baudelaire, Sterne, and Swift; and at least two uncollected poems, "Spiders" and "All Night, All Night," which were published in the *New Republic*. The book might also include a verse passage or two from *Shenandoah* and judicious selections from *Genesis*.

As a critic, Schwartz is almost always interesting and pertinent. He is at ease, generous, and free of didactic earnestness. His critical articles are at a more consistent level of excellence than his creative work, in part, as Philip Rahv suggests, because "the critical medium permits only a minimum of subjectivity."[41] The need to be objective saved him from incoherent self-reflectiveness, as it did in several poems that focus upon given forms—works of art, the styles of other men. Moreover, as it has been noted in comparing the heaviness of *Genesis* with the ease of his stories, Schwartz is usually at his best when he forgets to be earnest, when he allows himself to be nonchalant. "Regarding himself as a creative writer above all and therefore attaching no ultimate importance to articles and reviews," Rahv writes, "he was able to approach the writing of them with greater relaxation and, curiously enough, in a more disciplined spirit."[42]

Such a selection as suggested of Schwartz's creative work, together with the best of his critical articles, which have appeared in *Selected Essays*, would survive the poet's self-doubt—and, one hopes, the destruction of time, his great antagonist.

Notes and References

Chapter One

1. Philip Rahv, "Delmore Schwartz: The Paradox of Precocity," *New York Review of Books*, May 20, 1971, p. 20.

2. Alfred Kazin, "Delmore Schwartz, 1913–1966," *World Journal Tribune Book Week*, October 9, 1966, p. 17.

3. Maurice Zolotow says that Miss Wrinn "was the most important early influence in [Schwartz's] career and got him started writing verse and encouraged him." Information in a letter to the author, December 12, 1967.) His future wife, Gertrude Buckman, also appeared in both *The Poets' Pack* and *The Hollow Reed*.

4. Mary J. J. Wrinn, *The Hollow Reed* (New York and London, 1935), pp. 170–71.

5. *Ibid.*, p. 376.

6. *Choosing Company, The New Caravan*, ed. Alfred Kreymborg, Lewis Mumford, and Paul Rosenfeld (New York, 1936), p. 281.

7. *Ibid.*, p. 283.

8. One of five prizes awarded annually to graduate students for distinguished essays in several areas. The award consisted of a cash prize of $300 (now $700) and a bronze medal.

9. "Poetry as Imitation" (Harvard University Archives), pp. 3–4.

10. *Ibid.*, p. 5.

11. The review, originally associated with the American Communist party, was appearing again for the first time since October of the previous year, 1936, when its principal editors, William Phillips and Philip Rahv, suspended publication, partly because they lacked funds and partly because they had become disillusioned with Stalinism. They had always been dubious of party influence upon the policy of the magazine. Schwartz's story appears in sequence as the first contribution to the restored review, immediately following a statement of political and literary autonomy by Phillips, Rahv, and four new editors, including F. W. Dupee and Dwight Macdonald. For more information on the background of the magazine, consult William Phillips and Philip Rahv, "In Retrospect: Ten Years of *Partisan Review*," *The Partisan Reader*, ed. William Phillips and Philip Rahv (New York, 1946), pp. 679–88.

12. Philip Blair Rice, "The Rimbaud Mystery Clarified," *Poetry*, LVI (May, 1940), 101.

13. In a letter to Leonard C. van Geysel, May 24, 1940. *Letters of Wallace Stevens*, ed. Holly Stevens (New York, 1966), p. 356.

14. Roger Shattuck, "The Brother of Us All," *New York Review of Books*, June 1, 1967, p. 10.

15. "Adroitly Naïve," *Poetry*, XLVIII (May, 1936), 115–17.

16. "Defective Sincerity," *Poetry*, L (July, 1937), 233–36.

17. "A Note on the Nature of Art," *Marxist Quarterly*, I (April-June, 1937), 305–10.

18. Information in a letter to the author, May 8, 1969.

Chapter Two

1. "The Fiction of Ernest Hemingway," *Perspectives USA*, XIII (Autumn, 1955), 78.

2. "T. S. Eliot as the International Hero," *Partisan Review*, XII (Spring, 1945), 199–200.

3. *Ibid.*, p. 201.

4. *Ibid.*, p. 202.

5. *Ibid.*, p. 204.

6. Philip Rahv comments: "He wanted to be a great poet and because of this aspiration he was fascinated above all by T. S. Eliot's career—the paradigmatic instance of the success he craved. That he greatly admired Eliot's poetry goes without saying, but what struck me in his truly obsessive talk about Eliot was the note of suspicion it sounded, the elusive hints of literary politics and the gossipy stories that plainly had no foundation in fact about the man behind the career, a man, by the way, he had never known. There was something in these palpably absurd stories, abounding with 'delusions of reference,' . . . that contained in embryo the paranoia that later overwhelmed him." "Delmore Schwartz: The Paradox of Precocity," p. 21. Apparently the two poets never met, but Eliot on one occasion sent a letter of gratitude to Schwartz for an article he wrote on *The Criterion*, Eliot's magazine: "*The Criterion*, 1922-1939," *Kenyon Review*, I (Autumn, 1939), 437–49.

7. "T. S. Eliot as the International Hero," p. 206.

8. "The Isolation of Modern Poetry," *Kenyon Review*, III (Spring, 1941), 211.

9. *Ibid.*, pp. 212–13.

10. *Ibid.*, p. 214.

11. *Ibid.*, p. 217.

12. *Ibid.*, p. 218.

13. "T. S. Eliot's Voice and His Voices," *Poetry*, LXXXV (December, 1954), 172.

14. "The Vocation of the Poet in the Modern World," *Poetry*, LXXVIII (July, 1951), 225–26.

15. *Ibid.*, p. 229.

16. *Ibid.*, p. 231.

17. "Primitivism and Decadence," *Southern Review*, III (Winter, 1938), 608.

18. "Instructed of Much Mortality," *Sewanee Review*, LIV (Summer, 1946), 440–41.

19. *Ibid.*, p. 443.

20. *Genesis* (New York, 1943), p. viii.

21. "The Critical Method of R. P. Blackmur," *Poetry*, LIII (October, 1938), 36.

22. "The Meaningfulness of Absurdity," *Partisan Review*, XIII (Spring, 1946), 250.

23. "The Vocation of the Poet in the Modern World," p. 232.

24. "Under Forty," *Contemporary Jewish Record*, VII (February, 1944), 12.

25. *Ibid.*, p. 13.

26. *Ibid.*, p. 14. Harry Levin, who knew Schwartz when the poet was teaching at Harvard, writes that the poet regarded the university with unwarranted suspicion. "Clearly he never ceased to regard it, from his own parochial vantage-point, as enemy territory. He saw anti-Semitism everywhere." In conformity with his statement in the present article, Schwartz "maintained that he had never really experienced this blight until his graduate career." (Information in a letter to the author, August 5, 1970.)

27. *Ibid.*, p. 14.

28. *The World Is a Wedding* (Norfolk, Connecticut, 1948), p. 103.

29. *Ibid.*, p. 105.

30. Leslie Fiedler, "Zion as Main Street," *Waiting for the End* (New York, 1964), p. 66. Excellent survey of the emergence of Jewish American writers.

31. "Under Forty," p. 12.

Chapter Three

1. Heinz Politzer, "The Two Worlds of Delmore Schwartz," *Commentary*, X (December, 1950), 561–62.

2. In a number of instances Schwartz comments upon the relationship between his fiction and his life. In one of his notes to the text of *In Dreams Begin Responsibilities* he denies that the title story is autobiographical, inasmuch as no happening there ever took place. Though it is relevant to an important circumstance in his own life, the unhappy alliance of his mother and father, he is right in insisting that the story itself is an invention, wholly fictional in its *form*. Again, in a footnote to the story "America! America!" when it appeared (in a somewhat different version) in *Partisan Review*,

he says that "the characters in this story are not to be identified with any actual persons. This is a work of fiction in the full sense of the word." VII (March-April, 1940), 112. There can be no doubt, however, that the fictional hero, here as in other work, is a projection of his own self.

Most relevant is his comment in the preface to *Genesis*: "Since this narrative is a mixture throughout of invention and memory ... it is an obvious stupidity and misuse to take any sentence as the truth about any particular human being. I hope that there is in this work some truth about all human beings...." P. ix. The life is reinvented by means of art; what begins as the private and particular experience of the individual becomes universal. Though much of his work derives from his life, it would be wrong to accept specific details as documentary evidence, which would be to misrepresent his life and debase the imaginative function of his work.

3. *Selected Poems* (New York, 1967), pp. 132–33.

4. *Ibid.*, p. 67.

5. *Ibid.*, p. 58.

6. *Genesis*, p. 38.

7. *Selected Poems*, p. 46.

8. Kazin, "Delmore Schwartz, 1913–1966," p. 18.

9. *The World Is a Wedding*, p. 136.

10. *Ibid.*, pp. 138–39.

11. *Genesis*, p. 140.

12. *Ibid.*, p. 91.

13. *Ibid.*, p. 142.

14. *Selected Poems*, p. 196. It seems hardly necessary to say that light as symbolic of the mind and the spirit pervades literature. Snow as a symbol of peaceful oblivion is not uncommon. It appears as such at the end of "The Dead," Joyce's great story in *Dubliners*: "His soul swooned slowly as he heard the snow falling faintly through the universe and faintly falling, like the descent of their last end, upon all the living and the dead." In Robert Frost's "Stopping by Woods on a Snowy Evening," snowfall is invested with the same alluring power it had for Schwartz. As for the symbolism of whiteness, perhaps no one has defined it better than Herman Melville in his chapter "The Whiteness of the Whale," from *Moby Dick*. For Melville, however, whiteness represents values quite different from those that Schwartz assigns to it, whether conceived of as absence or presence: "... it is at once the most meaning symbol of spiritual things, nay, the very veil of the Christian's deity; and yet ... the intensifying agent in things the most appalling to mankind." Among these are the polar bear and the white shark, "transcendent horrors." Colors "are but subtle deceits ... laid on from without" by "the

great principle of light," which "for ever remains white or colorless in itself." On the one hand there is illusion, on the other a sinister, stark absolute.

15. *Shenandoah* (Norfolk, Connecticut, 1941), pp. 20–21.

16. "The Isolation of Modern Poetry," p. 216. The poem is "L'Etranger," from Baudelaire's *Spleen de Paris.*

17. Jean-Paul Sartre, *Baudelaire,* trans. Martin Turnell (New York, 1950), p. 143.

18. *Ibid.* Sartre's remarks on the past seen as destiny and art as a pseudoreligion seem pertinent enough, but they need qualification. Baudelaire was after all a defender and promoter of the living as well as the dead, of Wagner and Delacroix, for example; and in producing his own work he faced the challenges of art without flinching.

19. *Vaudeville for a Princess* (New York, 1950), p. 35.

20. *The World Is a Wedding,* p. 25.

21. *Selected Poems,* p. 37.

22. *Ibid.,* p. 38.

23. *Ibid.,* p. 52.

Chapter Four

1. By Joseph Gordon Macleod, from his poem "Libra, or, the Scales," in *The Ecliptic* (London, 1930), pp. 46–51.

2. William Butler Yeats, *The Collected Poems of William Butler Yeats* (New York, 1952), p. 98.

3. "The Poetry of Allen Tate," *Southern Review,* V (Winter, 1940), 431.

4. *Ibid.,* p. 426. Wallace Stevens remarks in his letter to Leonard C. van Geysel, May 24, 1940, that Schwartz "is extremely keen: perhaps too keen. After all, a poet has got to preserve feeling and, say what you will, thinking has a way of clearing up things from which feeling commonly arises: there is an antipathy between thinking and feeling." *Letters of Wallace Stevens,* p. 356.

5. *Selected Poems,* p. 30.

6. T. S. Eliot, *Collected Poems: 1909–1935* (New York, 1936), p. 129.

7. *Selected Poems,* p. 54.

8. Eliot, *Collected Poems: 1909–1935,* p. 43.

9. *Selected Poems,* pp. 21–24.

10. *Ibid.,* p. 25.

11. *Ibid.,* p. 30.

12. *Ibid.,* p. 29.

13. *Ibid.,* p. 30.

14. *Ibid.,* p. 32.

15. *Ibid.,* p. 33.
16. *Ibid.,* p. 34.
17. *Ibid.,* p. 41.
18. See H. D. Thoreau's *Walden,* Chapter 1: "The mass of men lead lives of quiet desperation. What is called resignation is confirmed desperation."
19. *Selected Poems,* pp. 43–44.
20. *Ibid.,* pp. 45–46.
21. *Ibid.,* p. 47.
22. *Ibid.,* p. 48.
23. *Ibid.,* p. 63.
24. *Ibid.,* p. 64.
25. *Ibid.,* p. 65.
26. *Ibid.,* pp. 66–67
27. *Ibid.,* p. 68.
28. *Ibid.,* pp. 69–70.
29. *Ibid.,* pp. 71–72.
30. *Ibid.,* p. 73.
31. *Ibid.,* pp. 74–75.
32. *Ibid.,* p. 76.
33. *Ibid.,* p. 77.

Chapter Five

1. *The World Is a Wedding,* p. 188.
2. *Ibid.,* p. 189.
3. *Ibid.,* p. 190.
4. *Ibid.,* p. 189.
5. *Ibid.,* p. 188.
6. *Ibid.,* p. 189.
7. *Ibid.,* p. 190.
8. *Ibid.,* p. 191.
9. *Ibid.,* p. 190.
10. *Ibid.,* p. 192.
11. *Ibid.,* p. 194.
12. *Ibid.*
13. *Ibid.,* pp. 194–95.
14. *Ibid.,* pp. 195–96.
15. *Selected Poems,* p. 90.
16. *Ibid.,* p. 81.
17. Freud was still living in 1938 when *Coriolanus and His Mother* was published, but apparently Schwartz regarded him as having already attained the status of the immortals.
18. *Selected Poems,* p. 99.
19. *Ibid.,* p. 142.

20. *Ibid.*, p. 85.
21. *Ibid.*, p. 126.
22. *Ibid.*, p. 84.
23. *The Tragedy of Coriolanus*, ed. Tucker Brooke (New Haven, 1924), p. 140.
24. *Selected Poems*, pp. 86–87.
25. *Ibid.*, pp. 88–90.
26. *Ibid.*, p. 124.
27. Louise Bogan, "Young Modern," *Nation*, CXLVIII (March 25, 1939), 354.
28. *Ibid.*
29. *The Tragedy of Coriolanus*, p. 20.
30. *Selected Poems*, pp. 87–88.
31. *Ibid.*, p. 90.
32. *The Tragedy of Coriolanus*, p. 30.
33. *In Dreams Begin Responsibilities* (Norfolk, Connecticut, 1938), pp. 142–43.
34. *Ibid.*, p. 144.
35. *Ibid.*, p. 149.
36. *Ibid.*, p. 151.
37. *Ibid.*, p. 154.
38. *Ibid.*, p. 156.
39. *Ibid.*, pp. 160–61.
40. *Ibid.*, p. 166.
41. *Ibid.*, p. 171.
42. Politzer, "The Two Worlds of Delmore Schwartz," p. 564.
43. Kazin, "Delmore Schwartz, 1913–1966," p. 18.
44. *Shenandoah* (Norfolk, Connecticut, 1941), pp. 7–9.
45. *Ibid.*, pp. 10–12.
46. *Ibid.*, p. 16.
47. *Ibid.*, p. 18.
48. *Ibid.*, p. 20.
49. *Ibid.*, pp. 24–27.
50. *Ibid.*, p. 28.
51. F. O. Matthiesen, "A New York Childhood," *Partisan Review*, X (May-June, 1943), 293.
52. *Genesis*, p. vii.
53. Matthiesen, "A New York Childhood," p. 293.
54. R. P. Blackmur, "Commentary by Ghosts," *Kenyon Review*, V (Summer, 1943), p. 468.
55. *Genesis*, p. 39.
56. *Ibid.*, p. 82.
57. *Ibid.*, p. 208.
58. *Ibid.*, p. 101.

59. *Ibid.*, p. 97.
60. *Ibid.*, p. 99.
61. *Ibid.*, pp. 14–15.
62. *Ibid.*, p. 78.
63. *Ibid.*, p. 166.
64. *Ibid.*, pp. 42–43.
65. *The World Is a Wedding*, p. 193.
66. *Genesis*, p. 54.
67. *Ibid.*, p. 118.
68. *Ibid.*, p. 91.
69. *Ibid.*, p. 140. See Chapter 3, p. 40.
70. *Ibid.*, p. 142.
71. *Ibid.*, pp. vii–viii.
72. "Poetry and Belief in Thomas Hardy," *Southern Review*, VI (Summer, 1940), 70–71.
73. *Ibid.*, pp. 72–73.
74. *Ibid.*, p. 73. In his preface to *Genesis* Schwartz quotes from Hardy's own preface to his *Dynasts* to support his method of having abstract ideas voiced by commentators. Hardy writes: "It was thought proper to introduce, as supernatural spectators of the terrestrial action, certain impersonated abstractions, or Intelligences, called Spirits. They are intended to be taken by the reader . . . as contrivances of the fancy merely. Their doctrines are but tentative. . . . The chief thing hoped for them is that they and their utterances may have dramatic plausibility. . . ." *The Dynasts* (London, 1926), p. viii.

This work, which prodigiously consists of nineteen acts and 130 scenes in prose and verse, is an "epic-drama," to use Hardy's own term, on the Napoleonic wars. The "impersonated abstractions" comment on the action singly or in chorus. Ironically, it seems highly possible that Schwartz as the writer of "Poetry and Belief in Thomas Hardy" would have regarded much of *The Dynasts* as exemplifying the failure that attended the poet when he betrayed his sensibility in favor of a "cosmological scene."
75. *Genesis*, p. 125.
76. Matthiesen, "A New York Childhood," p. 293.

Chapter Six

1. See pp. 29–30, 33–34, Chapter 2 for comments on this style.
2. Politzer, "The Two Worlds of Delmore Schwartz," p. 564.
3. Irving Howe, "Delmore Schwartz—A Personal Appreciation," *New Republic*, CXLVI (March 19, 1962), p. 25.
4. *The World Is a Wedding*, p. 118.
5. *Ibid.*, p. 112.

6. *Ibid.*
7. *Ibid.*, p. 116.
8. *Ibid.*, pp. 128–29.
9. *Ibid.*, p. 69.
10. *Ibid.*, p. 88.
11. *Ibid.*, p. 71.
12. *Ibid.*, p. 81.
13. *Ibid.*, p. 85.
14. *Ibid.*
15. *Ibid.*, pp. 86–87.
16. *Ibid.*, p. 88.
17. *Ibid.*, p. 89.
18. *Ibid.*, p. 160.
19. *Ibid.*, p. 147.
20. *Ibid.*, p. 145.
21. *Ibid.*, p. 178.
22. *Ibid.*, p. 186.
23. *Ibid.*
24. *Ibid.*, p. 187.
25. Politzer, "The Two Worlds of Delmore Schwartz," p. 564.
26. *The World Is a Wedding*, p. 18.
27. *Ibid.*, p. 15.
28. *Ibid.*, p. 10.
29. *Ibid.*, p. 9.
30. *Ibid.*, p. 18.
31. *Ibid.*, p. 11.
32. *Ibid.*, p. 38.
33. The Kafka story in question is "An Old Manuscript." As Rudyard reminds Laura, it is in fact about nomads who besiege a city and live on stolen butcher's meat. There is, however, an instance in the story of eating an ox alive. Laura is intent upon representing herself as a sacrificial victim.
34. *The World Is a Wedding*, p. 65.
35. *Ibid.*, p. 66.
36. *Ibid.*, p. 68.
37. Politzer, "The Two Worlds of Delmore Schwartz," p. 565.

Chapter Seven

1. Rolfe Humphries, "A Verse Chronicle," *Nation*, CLXXI (November 25, 1950), 490.
2. *Vaudeville for a Princess* (New York, 1950), p. 1.
3. *Ibid.*, p. 65.
4. Joseph Bennett, "Five Books, Four Poets," *Hudson Review*, IV (Spring, 1951), 138.

5. *Vaudeville for a Princess,* p. 3. The sentence in question is from Pascal's *Pensées:* "*La vraye éloquence se moque de l'éloquence.*"

6. *Ibid.,* pp. 7–8.

7. Sir Edward Dyer, "My Mind to Me a Kingdom Is," in J. William Hebel and Hoyt H. Hudson, eds., *Poetry of the English Renaissance, 1509–1660* (New York, 1929), p. 123.

8. *Vaudeville for a Princess,* pp. 13–14.

9. *Ibid.,* p. 20.

10. William Wordsworth, *Selected Poetry,* ed. Mark Van Doren (New York, 1950), p. 468.

11. *Vaudeville for a Princess,* pp. 27–28.

12. *Ibid.,* pp. 34–36.

13. *Ibid.,* pp. 47-49, or *Selected Poems,* pp. 238–40.

14. *Ibid.,* p. 58.

15. *Ibid.,* pp. 60–61.

16. *Ibid.,* p. 63.

17. Humphries, "A Verse Chronicle," p. 490.

18. *Vaudeville for a Princess,* p. 69.

19. *Ibid.,* p. 77.

20. *Ibid.,* p. 4.

21. *Ibid.,* p. 5.

22. *Ibid.,* p. 6.

23. *Ibid.,* p. 10.

24. *Ibid.,* p. 29.

25. *Ibid.,* pp. 25–26.

26. *Ibid.,* p. 16.

27. *Ibid.,* p. 19.

28. *Ibid.,* pp. 45–46.

29. *Ibid.,* p. 40.

Chapter Eight

1. *Selected Poems,* p. 193.

2. *Ibid.,* p. 177.

3. *Ibid.,* p. 169.

4. *Ibid.,* p. 174.

5. *Ibid.,* p. 152.

6. *Ibid.*

7. *Ibid.*

8. *Ibid.,* pp. 152–53.

9. *Ibid.,* p. 153.

10. *Ibid.,* pp. 154–55.

11. *Ibid.,* pp. 155–56.

12. *Ibid.,* pp. 150–51.

13. *Ibid.,* pp. 157–58.

14. *Ibid.,* pp. 194–95.

15. Information in a letter to the author, June 17, 1968. In the same letter Professor Schapiro suggests a biographical reason for Schwartz's liking Seurat's painting: "It may be that Delmore's delight in the *Sunday on the Grande Jatte* had to do also with memories of childhood, when the park and the Sunday stroll were an experience of the idyllic, the only opening to arcadian joys in the big city." Schapiro also notes that "there is in Seurat's painting an aspect of the comic, the whimsical and Gothic in the silhouettes . . . which appealed to Delmore's alert sense of humor."

16. Meyer Schapiro, "New Light on Seurat," *Art News,* LVII (April, 1958), 44–45. Schwartz's poem is dedicated to Schapiro and his wife Lillian. He was influenced by the article, passages of which he re-creates in the poem. He also attended a lecture by Schapiro on Seurat several years earlier.

17. *Selected Poems,* p. 196.

18. *Ibid.,* p. 190.

19. *Ibid.,* p. 192.

20. *Ibid.,* pp. 190–91.

21. *Ibid.,* p. 192.

22. *Ibid.,* p. 195.

23. *Ibid.,* p. 196.

24. *Ibid.* These lines refer to a passage in the biography of Kafka by his friend Max Brod: ". . . writing, of however high a standard, was not enough according to Kafka's lights. . . . I shall never forget the deep emotion with which Kafka read to me a paragraph of *Souvenirs Intimes* by Flaubert's niece, Caroline Commanville." To summarize Brod's account of this, Madame Commanville tells of a visit she and her uncle paid to a happy middle-class family of her acquaintance, and how Flaubert, who had sacrificed his life to literature, afterward expressed his envious admiration of their normal existence. "As they were walking home along the Seine, Flaubert said, '*Ils sont dans le vrai.*'" Kafka, says Brod, "often quoted this sentence. Art alone then had not been enough for him. . . ." Max Brod, *Franz Kafka: A Biography,* trans. G. Humphreys Roberts (New York, 1947), p. 98. Flaubert's remark, literally "They are in the truth," might be rendered, "They are right," or, "Theirs is the right way."

25. *Ibid.,* p. 173.

26. *Ibid.,* p. 174.

27. *Ibid.,* p. 175.

28. *Ibid.,* p. 180.

29. *Ibid.,* p. 181.

30. *Ibid.,* p. 185.

31. Laurence Sterne, *Letters of Laurence Sterne,* ed. Lewis Perry Curtis (London, 1935), p. 335.

32. *Selected Poems,* p. 180.

33. Sterne, *Letters of Laurence Sterne,* p. 337.

34. *Selected Poems,* p. 187.

35. *Ibid.,* p. 188.

36. *Ibid.*

37. *Ibid.,* p. 176.

38. *Ibid.,* p. 161.

39. Two uncollected late poems listed in the bibliography call for special mention here: "Spiders" and "All Night, All Night," which appeared in the *New Republic* in 1959 and 1960, respectively.

40. *Selected Poems,* p. 217.

41. Rahv, "Delmore Schwartz: The Paradox of Precocity," p. 21.

42. *Ibid.*

Selected Bibliography

PRIMARY SOURCES

1. Collected Poetry, Fiction, and Criticism
In Dreams Begin Responsibilities. Norfolk, Connecticut: New Directions, 1938.
A Season in Hell. Norfolk, Connecticut: New Directions, 1939. A translation of *Une Saison en Enfer*, by Arthur Rimbaud. Second edition, 1940.
Shenandoah. Norfolk, Connecticut: New Directions, 1941. A shorter version of this play appeared in *Kenyon Review*, III (Summer, 1941), 271–92, entitled *Shenandoah, Or, the Naming of the Child*. Anthologies are:
   Poetic Drama, ed. Alfred Kreymborg. New York: Modern Age Books, 1941, pp. 842–52.
   Modern American Poetry, ed. Louis Untermeyer, New York: Harcourt, Brace and Company, 1950, pp. 619–20. A selection, entitled "Let Us Consider Where the Great Men Are."
Genesis: Book I. New York: New Directions, 1943.
The World Is a Wedding. Norfolk, Connecticut: New Directions, 1948. All of these stories appeared first in magazines and some have been anthologized, as follows:
   "In Dreams Begin Responsibilities," *Partisan Review*, IV (December, 1937), 5–11. Reprinted in the more recent anthologies: *The Expanded Moment*, ed. Robert Gordon. Boston: D. C. Heath and Company, 1963, pp. 159–65; *Contemporary American Short Stories*, ed. Douglas Angus and Sylvia Angus. New York: Fawcett Publications, Inc., 1967, pp. 222–29; *Short Stories, Classic, Modern, Contemporary*, ed. Marcus Klein and Robert Pack. Boston: Little, Brown and Company, 1967, pp. 383–92.
   "The Statues," *Partisan Review*, IV (May, 1938), 11–18.
   "America! America!" *Partisan Review*, VII (March-April, 1940), 112–34. Reprinted in *The Partisan Review Anthology*, ed. William Phillips and Philip Rahv. New York: Holt, Rinehart and Winston, 1962, pp. 283–99.
   "New Year's Eve," *Partisan Review*, XII (Summer, 1945), 327–44.
   "A Bitter Farce," *Kenyon Review*, VIII (Spring, 1946), 245–61.

Reprinted in *A Treasury of American Jewish Stories*, ed. Harold Uriel Ribalow. New York: Thomas Yoseloff, 1958, pp. 264–80.

"The Child Is the Meaning of This Life," *Partisan Review*, XIV (May–June, 1947), 255–77, and (July–August, 1947), 352–70.

"The World Is a Wedding," *Partisan Review*, XV (March, 1948), 279–87. Parts 1 and 2 only.

Vaudeville for a Princess and Other Poems. New York: New Directions, 1950. Many items of this collection appeared first in magazines, and some were reprinted in anthologies. The following are worthy of special note:

"The True, the Good, and the Beautiful," *Partisan Review*, XIV (March–April, 1947), 146–49. An earlier version. Reprinted in *Mid-Century American Poets*, ed. John Ciardi. New York: Twayne Publishers, Inc., 1950, pp. 291–94.

"Existentialism: The Inside Story." Appeared as "Does Existentialism Still Exist?" *Partisan Review*, XV (December, 1948), 1361–63.

"Lunas Are Tempting to Old Consciousness," *Nation*, CLXXI (September 16, 1950), 251. Reprinted in *One Hundred Years of the Nation*, ed. Henry M. Christman. New York: The Macmillan Company, 1965, pp. 368–69.

Summer Knowledge: New and Selected Poems, 1938–1958. Garden City, New York: Doubleday and Company, Inc., 1959.

Successful Love and Other Stories. New York: Corinth Books, 1961.

Selected Poems (1938–1958): Summer Knowledge. New York: New Directions, 1967. A paperback reprint of *Summer Knowledge*.

Selected Essays of Delmore Schwartz, ed. Donald A. Dike and David H. Zucker. Chicago: The University of Chicago Press, 1970.

For Delmore Schwartz's earliest published poems, see WRINN, MARY J. J. *The Hollow Reed*. New York and London: Harper and Brothers, Publishers, 1935. A poetry textbook by one of Schwartz's English teachers at high school; contains five of his poems.

2. Uncollected Poetry and Fiction. Unless noted otherwise, the works listed are poems.

"Aubade," *Mosaic*, I (November–December, 1934), 9.

Choosing Company. The New Caravan. Ed. Alfred Kreymborg, Lewis Mumford, and Paul Rosenfeld. New York: W. W. Norton and Company, Inc., 1936, pp. 271–89. Play in verse and prose.

"Poem," *Poetry*, XLIX (February, 1937), 252.

"Poem," *Poetry*, XLIX (February, 1937), 252–53.

"The Commencement Day Address," *New Directions in Prose and Poetry 1937*. Ed. James Laughlin. Norfolk, Connecticut: New Directions, 1937, no pagination. Short story.

"Metro-Goldwyn-Mayer," *New Directions in Prose and Poetry 1937*. Ed. James Laughlin. Norfolk, Connecticut: New Directions, 1937, no pagination.

"The Heart, a Black Grape Gushing Hidden Streams," *Poetry*, LI (January, 1938), 199.

Paris and Helen, New Directions in Prose and Poetry 1941. Ed. James Laughlin. Norfolk, Connecticut: New Directions, 1941, pp. 193–218. Verse play.

"An Argument in 1934," *Kenyon Review*, IV (Winter, 1942), 62–74. Short story.

"Poem," *Commentary*, XXV (May, 1958), 400.

"Sonnet," *Commentary*, XXV (May, 1958), 400.

"Kilroy's Carnival: A Poetic Prologue for T. V.," *New Republic*, CXXXIX (December 1, 1958), 15–16.

"Spiders," *New Republic*, CXLI (July 6, 1959), 18.

"Passages from the Studies of Narcissus," *Chicago Review*, XIII (Summer, 1959), 121–23.

"Philology Recapitulates Ontology, Poetry is Ontology," *Prairie Schooner*, XXXIII (Summer, 1959), 154.

"Poem," *Prairie Schooner*, XXXIII (Summer, 1959), 155.

"Song," *Prairie Schooner*, XXXIII (Summer, 1959), 156.

"The Choir and Music of Solitude and Silence," *New Republic*, CXLI (September 28, 1959), 27.

"Poem," *New Republic*, CXLI (October 19, 1959), 24.

"All Night, All Night," *New Republic*, CXLII (March 21, 1960), 18.

"This Is a Poem I Wrote at Night, Before the Dawn," *New Republic*, CXLV (October 23, 1961), 24.

"Words for a Trumpet Chorale Celebrating the Autumn," *New Republic*, CXLV (November 13, 1961), 12.

"Aria," *New Republic*, CXLVI (April 23, 1962), 26.

"Journey of a Poem Compared to All the Sad Variety of Travel," *Kenyon Review*, XXIV (Spring, 1962), 304.

"Poem," *New Republic*, CXLVII (July 16, 1962), 21.

"Apollo Musagete, Poetry, and the Leader of the Muses," *Poetry*, CI (October–November, 1962), 108–11.

"Two Lyrics from Kilroy's Carnival: A Masque," *Sewanee Review*, LXX (Winter, 1962), 12–13.

3. Selected Critical Articles and Reviews

"New Verse," *Partisan Review*, IV (February, 1938), 49–52. Appreciative review of *The Man with the Blue Guitar,* by Wallace Stevens.

"Primitivism and Decadence," *Southern Review,* III (Winter, 1938), 597–614. Review of *Primitivism and Decadence: A Study of American Experimental Poetry,* by Yvor Winters. Discusses Winters' tenet that the writing of a poem is a moral act; the nature of belief in poetry; the means whereby a writer avoids "the fallacy of imitative form."

"Ezra Pound's Very Useful Labors," *Poetry,* LI (March, 1938), 324–29. Favorable review of Pound's *Fifth Decad of Cantos.*

"Ernest Hemingway's Literary Situation," *Southern Review,* III (Spring, 1938), 769–82. Discusses the importance of sensation and conduct in Hemingway's work. Hemingway's failure as a social critic in *To Have and To Have Not.*

"The Critical Method of R. P. Blackmur," *Poetry,* LIII (October, 1938), 28–39. Review of Blackmur's *Double Agent.* Phrases what he believes to be the "essential canon" of Blackmur. Touches upon the relation between form and substance and the place of belief in poetry.

"John Dos Passos and the Whole Truth," *Southern Review,* IV (Autumn, 1938), 351–67. Review of Dos Passos *U.S.A.* Critical of the method of naturalism. Believes Dos Passos has failed: "His novel is perhaps the greatest monument of naturalism because it betrays so fully the poverty and disintegration inherent in that method."

"The Poet As Poet," *Partisan Review,* VI (Spring, 1939), 52–59. One of two essays on William Butler Yeats, the other by W. H. Auden, under the general title "The Public v. the Late Mr. William Butler Yeats." Great praise for Yeats, who is considered as a poet who began as a romantic, but "shifted from the effort to write 'poetic' poetry of the 'Nineties to the concern . . . with what it was to be a poet amid the alien circumstances of his age."

"Rimbaud in Our Time," *Poetry* LV (December, 1939), 148–54. An article that served as the basis for his introduction to his translation of *Une Saison en Enfer.* Critical of capitalism.

"The Poetry of Allen Tate," *Southern Review,* V (Winter, 1940), 419–38. Review of Tate's *Selected Poems.* Tate as an intellectual poet with a traditional outlook.

"Poetry and Belief in Thomas Hardy," *Southern Review,* VI (Summer, 1940), 64–77. On the function of belief in poetry, as exemplified by Hardy's poems.

"The Ultimate Plato with Picasso's Guitar," *Harvard Advocate,* CXXVII (December, 1940), 11–16. On Wallace Stevens, whom he calls an "aesthete in the best sense of the word." The entire issue is devoted to an appraisal of Stevens.

"The Isolation of Modern Poetry," *Kenyon Review,* III (Spring, 1941), 209–20. Survey of the causes of the poet's isolation in the modern world.

"The Fiction of William Faulkner," *Southern Review* (Summer, 1941), 145–60. Admires Faulkner; deplores what he thinks to be his neglect of reading and lack of self-criticism.

"An Unwritten Book," *Southern Review,* VII (Winter, 1942), 471–91. Brilliant essay on William Butler Yeats; approaches the poet "by taking some of the questions, problems, and mysteries which Yeats makes inevitable and considering them under the figure of an unwritten book, the unwritten book about Yeats which would tell the whole truth about him; or if not the whole truth, the truth we need to hear."

"The Poetry of Millay," *Nation,* CLVII (December 18, 1943), 735–36. Generally disapproving review of *Collected Lyrics,* by Edna St. Vincent Millay.

"Under Forty," *Contemporary Jewish Record,* VII (February, 1944), 12–14. One of several articles for "A Symposium on American Literature and the Younger Generation of Jews."

"T. S. Eliot As the International Hero," *Partisan Review,* XII (Spring, 1945), 199–206. Eliot as a "culture hero."

"The Dream from Which No One Awakes," *Nation,* CXLI (December 1, 1945), 590–93. Favorable review of *Little Friend, Little Friend,* by Randall Jarrell.

"The Meaningfulness of Absurdity," *Partisan Review,* XIII (Spring, 1946), 246–50. Review of works by Albert Camus, among them *Le Mythe de Sisyphe, Essai sur l'absurde,* and *Le Malentendu.* Camus as a writer of ideas.

"Instructed of Much Mortality," *Sewanee Review,* LIV (Summer, 1946), 439–48. Praise for the poetry of John Crowe Ransom and Wallace Stevens, with a discussion of their styles.

"Auden and Stevens," *Partisan Review,* XIV (September–October, 1947), 528–32. Review of *The Age of Anxiety,* by W. H. Auden and *Transport to Summer,* by Wallace Stevens. Adverse criticism of Auden's book; praise for Stevens.

"The Literary Dictatorship of T. S. Eliot," *Partisan Review,* XVI (February, 1949), 119–37. Extensive essay on T. S. Eliot; estimates his weaknesses and strengths as a critic.

"Views of a Second Violinist," *Partisan Review,* XVI (December, 1949), 1250–55. On the obscurity of modern poetry and the problems of the modern poet.

"The Vocation of the Poet in the Modern World," *Poetry,* LXXVIII

(July, 1951), 223–32. On the poet's use of the modern idiom. The international quality of modern life and its effect upon language. Joyce and Eliot as international writers. Identification of the artist with the Jew.

"Fiction Chronicle: Dear Uncle James," *Partisan Review*, XIX (March–April, 1952), 234–38. Reviews of books by John Don Passos, John O'Hara, and Graham Greene in the form of an imaginary letter to James Joyce.

"Masterpieces As Cartoons," *Partisan Review*, XIX (July, 1952), 461–71. Attack on comic books based on great works of fiction.

"Our Country and Our Culture," *Partisan Review*, XIX (September, 1952), 593–97. Last contribution to a symposium published in a three-part series. Schwartz advocates critical nonconformism.

"The Duchess' Red Shoes," *Partisan Review*, XX (January–February, 1953), 55–73. Article on manners in the novel, which refers to a commentary by John W. Aldridge that appeared in the May–June issue of the magazine, and to the essay "Manners, Morals, and the Novel," by Lionel Trilling, from his collection, *The Liberal Imagination*. The article began a controversy that was carried on in a correspondence between Schwartz and Paul Ramsey, Jr., in the May–June, 1953 issue of *Partisan Review* ("Manners and Morals," pp. 362–68) and continued by Aldridge in an essay in his *In Search of Heresy* (See under Secondary Sources, 1).

"Adventure in America," *Partisan Review*, XXI (January–February, 1954), 112–15. Review of *The Adventures of Augie March*, by Saul Bellow.

"T. S. Eliot's Voice and His Voices," *Poetry*, LXXXV (December, 1954), 170–76, and (January, 1955), 232–42. On Eliot's use of prosaic words in his poetry, and his "poetic and creative use of the printed word and of his reading not only as a source of inspiration but as the material of the actual poem." Eliot as a poet of "many voices," whose poems "are often dominated by a *listening* to other voices," which becomes a formal principle.

"William Faulkner's 'A Fable,'" *Perspectives USA*, X (Winter, 1955), 126–36. A detailed appraisal of the novel in question.

"The Fiction of Ernest Hemingway," *Perspectives USA*, XIII (Autumn, 1955), 70–78. Astute remarks on Hemingway's personality and his literary reputation.

"The Present State of Modern Poetry," *American Poetry at Mid-Century*. Washington: The Library of Congress, 1958, pp. 15–31. Speaks of the state of poetry at the time of his youth and changes since: the popularity of poetry readings; the establishment of the poet at the university. Discounts the revolutionary claims of the San Francisco poets emerging at the time of this article, and comments upon "the tameness and restrained calm" of the academic poets. Probably Schwartz's last published critical work of any importance.

SECONDARY SOURCES

1. Books

ALDRIDGE, JOHN W. *In Search of Heresy*. Port Washington, New York: Kennikat Press, Inc., 1967, pp. 39, 77–87. Contributes to the argument provoked by Schwartz's *Partisan Review* article, "The Duchess' Red Shoes."

MALIN, IRVING. *Jews and Americans*. Carbondale and Edwardsville: Southern Illinois University Press, 1965. Examines the work of Schwartz and six other Jewish American writers in relation to various themes. Interesting but often perfunctory.

NYREN, DOROTHY. *A Library of Literary Criticism*. New York: Frederick Ungar Publishing Company, 1960, pp. 436–41. Selection of abstracts from book reviews and articles about Schwartz from 1939 to 1950.

ROSENTHAL, M. L. *The Modern Poets: A Critical Introduction*. New York: Oxford University Press, 1965. Survey of modern poetry; numerous references to Schwartz.

STEVENS, WALLACE. *The Letters of Wallace Stevens*. Ed. Holly Stevens. New York: Alfred A. Knopf, 1966. Contains three letters to Schwartz and several references to him in letters to other correspondents.

2. Articles, Essays, and Reviews

AIKEN, CONRAD. "Back to Poetry," *Atlantic Monthly*, CLXVI (August, 1940), 217–40. Reprinted in his *Reviewer's ABC*. London: W. H. Allen, 1961, pp. 355–58. Mention of Schwartz and Dylan Thomas as "the most satisfactory poets of the moment." Praise for *Coriolanus and His Mother*.

BLACKMUR, R. P. "Commentary by Ghosts," *Kenyon Review*, V (Summer, 1943), 467–71. Perceptive review of *Genesis*.

BOGAN, LOUISE. "Young Modern," *Nation*, CXLVIII (March 25, 1939), 353–54. Review of *In Dreams Begin Responsibilities*. Finds many of the lyrics imitative in manner; has unreserved praise for the title story.

BONHAM, SISTER M. HILDA. "Delmore Schwartz: An Idea of the World," *Renascence*, XIII (Spring, 1961), 132–35. Analysis of "The Heavy Bear Who Goes With Me."

CARRUTH, HAYDEN. "Comment," *Poetry*, CXII (September, 1968), 417–27. Contains a review of *Selected Poems* (or *Summer Knowledge*). There is "a great deal of bad poetry," as well as "perfect poems that rise here and there . . . like wild roses in a bank of weeds."

DEUTSCH, BABETTE. "Two Decades of Verse," *New York Times Book Review*, August 16, 1959, p. 22. Generally sympathetic review of *Summer Knowledge* (or *Selected Poems*).

————. "Useful Entertainment," *New York Herald Tribune Books*, March 5, 1939, p. 21. Review of *In Dreams Begin Responsibilities*. Annoyed by traces of Kafka, Yeats, and Auden; praises Schwartz's "sensibility" and "intelligence" in his best work.

DEUTSCH, R. H. "Poetry and Belief in Delmore Schwartz," *Sewanee Review*, LXXIV (Autumn, 1966), 915–24. Stresses the omnivorous ego of Schwartz.

FLINT, ROBERT W. "The Stories of Delmore Schwartz," *Commentary*, XXXIII (April, 1962), 336–39. Perceptive, thorough critique of Schwartz's stories.

HALIO, JAY L. "Delmore Schwartz's Felt Abstractions," *Southern Review*, I (Autumn, 1965), 802–19. Remarks on the differences between Schwartz's early poems and his later poems; notes predominance of "kinesthetic imagery" and "imagery of touch" in the first, and the presence of the concrete and the abstract in a state of balance. In the later stage, "light floods his poetry, replacing in large part the tactile abstractions. . . ."

HOWE, IRVING. "Delmore Schwartz—A Personal Appreciation," *New Republic*, CXLVI (March 19, 1962), 25–27. Appraises Schwartz's attempt to convert his experience as a Jew into fiction and describes the function of his ironic style.

HUMPHRIES, ROLFE. "A Verse Chronicle," *Nation*, CLXXI (November 25, 1950), 490. Best and fairest review of *Vaudeville for a Princess*.

JARRELL, RANDALL, "Contemporary Poetry Criticism," *New Republic*, CV (July 21, 1941), 88–90. Believes that Schwartz is in the company of the best modern critics.

KAZIN, ALFRED. "Delmore Schwartz, 1913–1966," *World Journal Tribune Book Week*, October 9, 1966, 1, 17–18. Interesting memoir of Schwartz in his last years with a discussion of his work.

KENNER, HUGH. "Bearded Ladies and the Abundant Goat," *Poetry*, LXXIX (October, 1951), 50–53. Unfavorable review of *Vaudeville for a Princess*.

LEIBOWITZ, HERBERT. "Selected Essays of Delmore Schwartz," *New York Times Book Review*, January 17, 1971, pp. 3, 33. Review of Schwartz's essays; excellent appraisal of Schwartz as a critic.

MACDONALD, DWIGHT. "Delmore Schwartz (1913–1966)," *New York Review of Books,* September 8, 1966, pp. 14–16. Memoir.

MATTHIESEN, F. O. "A New York Childhood," *Partisan Review,* X (May–June, 1943), 292–94. Reprinted in his *Responsibilities of a Critic.* Ed. John Rackcliffe. New York: Oxford University Press, 1952, pp. 112–15. Favorable review of *Genesis;* considered as a *Bildungsroman.*

O'BRIEN, JUSTIN. "A Mystic in the Raw," *Kenyon Review,* II (Spring, 1940), 229–32. Censure of Schwartz's translation, *A Season in Hell.*

O'CONNOR, WILLIAM VAN. "The Albatross Was Intended to Fly," *Poetry,* LXXIX (October, 1951), 55–59. Qualified praise for *Vaudeville for a Princess.*

O'DONNELL, G. M. "Delmore Schwartz's Achievement," *Poetry,* LIV (May, 1939), 105–8. High praise for *In Dreams Begin Responsibilities.*

POLITZER, HEINZ. "The Two Worlds of Delmore Schwartz: Lucifer in Brooklyn." Trans. Martin Greenberg. *Commentary,* X (December, 1950), 561–68. Most comprehensive study of the principal themes of Schwartz's work accomplished at the date of the article.

RAHV, PHILIP. "Delmore Schwartz: The Paradox of Precocity," *New York Review of Books,* May 20, 1971, pp. 19–22. Memoir by a friend and colleague that emphasizes Schwartz's precocity, especially as a critic, and discusses his personality.

ROSENTHAL, M. L. "Deep in the Unfriendly City," *Nation,* CXC (June 11, 1960), 515–16. Perceptive review of *Summer Knowledge* (or *Selected Poems*). Discusses Auden's influence upon the early poems. Of the later poems: "I do not make excuses for this section, but I have the impression from it that the poet has passed through a great spiritual change and is slowly finding his way in a new world."

VAN DOREN, MARK. "Music of a Mind," *Kenyon Review,* I (Spring, 1939), 208–11. Among the more enthusiastic reviews of *In Dreams Begin Responsibilities.*

3. Poems about Delmore Schwartz

BERRYMAN, JOHN. "At Chinese Checkers," *Short Poems.* New York: Farrar, Straus and Giroux, 1967, pp. 37–41. An early poem, dated 1939, that contains a description of Schwartz (p. 40): "Deep in the unfriendly city Delmore lies/ And cannot sleep, and cannot bring his mind/ And cannot bring those marvellous faculties/ To bear upon the day. . . ."

————. *His Toy, His Dream, His Rest*. New York: Farrar, Straus
and Giroux, Inc., 1968, pp. 75-86. Ten "dream songs" composing
a memoir of the poet. The book is dedicated "To Mark Van
Doren, and to the sacred memory of Delmore Schwartz."

LOWELL, ROBERT. "To Delmore Schwartz." *Life Studies*. New York:
Farrar, Straus and Cudahy, 1959, pp. 53–54. A memory of a
night spent with the poet at his home in Cambridge in 1946.

SCHAPIRO, MEYER. An untitled commemoration. *New York Review
of Books*, September 8, 1966, p. 15.

SHAPIRO, HARVEY. "For Delmore Schwartz," *Poetry*, CX (June,
1967), 160–61.

4. Obituary

"Delmore Schwartz Dies at 52; Poet Won 1959 Bollingen Prize,"
New York Times, July 14, 1966, p. 35.

Index

153